THE YEAR YOU WERE BORN
1963

A fascinating book about the year 1963 with information on:
Events of the year UK, Adverts of 1963, Cost of living, Births, Deaths, Sporting events, Book publications, Movies, Music, World events and People in power.

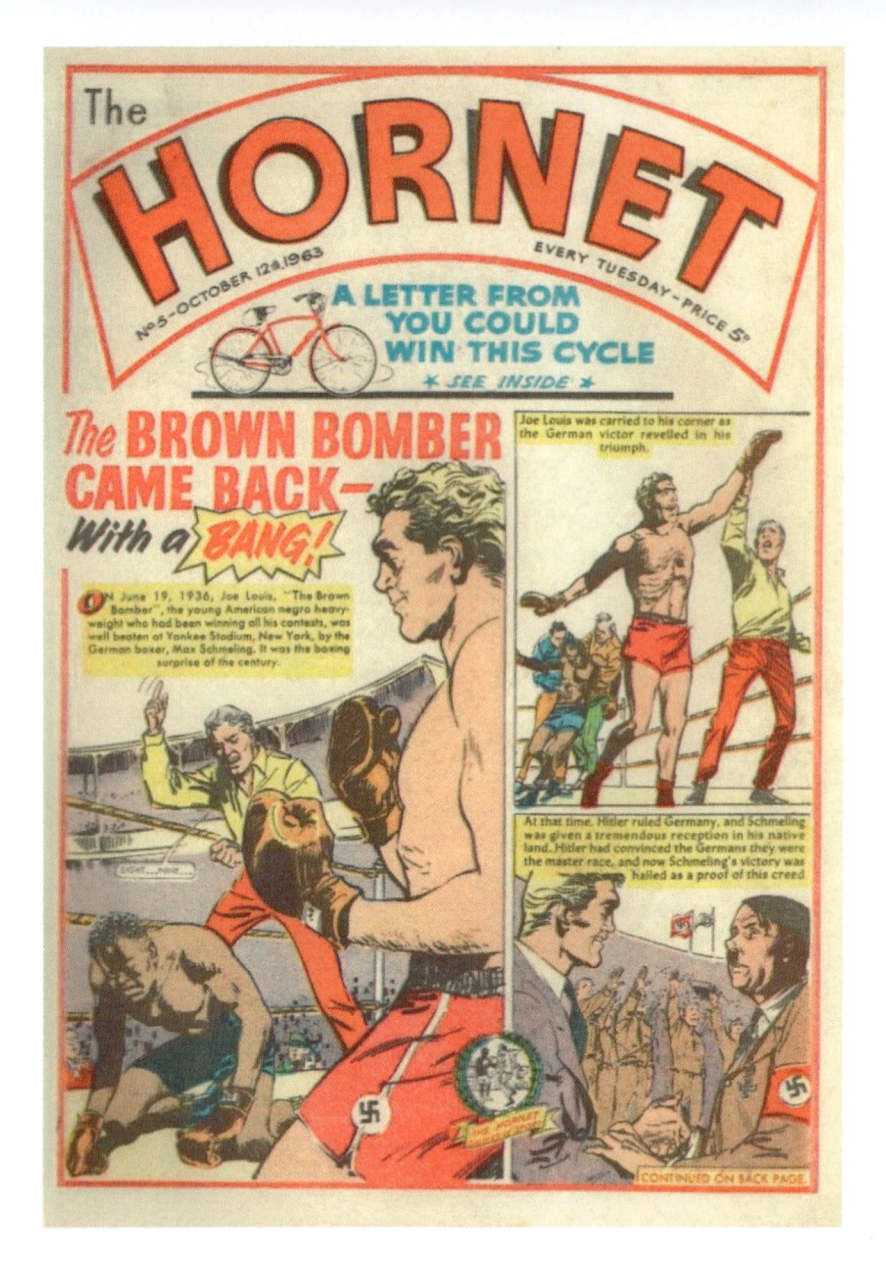

INDEX

Page 3   **Events of the year UK**
Page 19 **Adverts in 1963**
Page 26 **Cost of living**
Page 29 **Births**
Page 34 **Deaths**
Page 33 **Sporting events**
Page 43 **Book Publications**
Page 46 **Movies**
Page 56 **Music**
Page 65 **World Events**
Page 83 **People in power**

UK EVENTS OF 1963

January

1st | Winter of 1963: The UK experiences the worst winter since 1946–47. Low temperatures keep snow lying around until early-April in some areas. The winter of 1962–1963, known as the Big Freeze of 1963, was one of the coldest winters (defined as the months of December, January and February) on record in the United Kingdom. Temperatures plummeted and lakes and rivers began to freeze over. With an average temperature of −2.1 °C (28.2 °F), January 1963 remains the coldest month since January 1814 in Central England, although for the UK as a whole and in Northern England, Scotland and Northern Ireland. In January 1963, the sea froze for one mile (1.6 km) from shore at Herne Bay, Kent. The sea froze inshore in many places, removing many British inland waterbirds' usual last resort of finding food in estuaries and shallow sea. The sea froze 4 miles (6 km) out to sea from Dunkirk. The upper reaches of the River Thames froze over, although it did not freeze in Central London, partly due to the hot effluent from two thermal power stations, Battersea and Bankside. The removal of the multi-arched London Bridge, which had obstructed the river's free flow, and the addition of the river embankments, kept the river from freezing in London as it had in earlier times.

3rd | The Beatles begin their first tour of 1963 with a five-day tour in Scotland to support the release of their new single, "Love Me Do", beginning with a performance in Elgin.

4th | Decca records Benjamin Britten conducting his 1962 War Requiem with the soloists he originally composed it for: Galina Vishnevskaya, Peter Pears and Dietrich Fischer-Dieskau together with the London Symphony Orchestra and The Bach Choir, in London. Within five months of its release the recording sells 200,000 copies, an unheard-of number for a piece of contemporary classical music at this time.

6th | Alan Freeman takes over as presenter of Pick of the Pops; he remains with the programme until the BBC ceases to broadcast it in 1972, and then with revivals.

7th | Granada Television first broadcasts World in Action, its influential investigative current affairs series, which will run for thirty-five years.

January

11th	Musical film Summer Holiday starring Cliff Richard premieres in London. Summer Holiday is a 1963 British CinemaScope and Technicolor musical film starring singer Cliff Richard. The film was directed by Peter Yates (his directorial debut), produced by Kenneth Harper. The original screenplay was written by Peter Myers and Ronald Cass (who also wrote most of the song numbers and lyrics). The cast stars Lauri Peters, David Kossoff, Ron Moody and The Shadows and features Melvyn Hayes, Teddy Green, Jeremy Bulloch, Una Stubbs, Pamela Hart, Jacqueline Daryl, Madge Ryan, Lionel Murton, Christine Lawson, Wendy Barry and Nicholas Phipps. The John Lennon single "Please Please Me" is released by The Beatles in the UK, with "Ask Me Why" as the B-side.
12th	Spin bowler Bobby Simpson takes 5-57 for Australia v England.
13th	The play Madhouse on Castle Street is broadcast in the BBC Sunday-Night Play strand. Little-known young American folk music singer Bob Dylan had originally been cast as the lead but proved unsatisfactory as an actor and the play has been restructured to give him a singing role; he gives one of the earliest public performances of "Blowin' in the Wind" over the credits.
16th	The Macmillan-led Conservative government announces that a new town will be developed in Shropshire. Dawley New Town will incorporate existing communities including: Dawley, Ironbridge and Madeley, and will largely be used as an overspill town for Birmingham and Wolverhampton.
18th	The Labour Party leader, Hugh Gaitskell, dies suddenly aged 56.
23rd	Double agent Kim Philby disappears from Beirut having defected to the Soviet Union.
29th	Charles de Gaulle, President of France, vetoes the UK's entry into the European Economic Community.

February

1st The Royal Air Force deploys Blue Steel nuclear standoff missiles to arm its V bomber force. The Avro Blue Steel was a British air-launched, rocket-propelled nuclear armed standoff missile, built to arm the V bomber force. It allowed the bomber to launch the missile against its target while still outside the range of surface-to-air missiles (SAMs). The missile proceeded to the target at speeds up to Mach 3, and would trigger within 100 m of the pre-defined target point.

2nd The Beatles went on tour at the bottom of an eight-act bill headed by 16-year-old singer Helen Shapiro.

4th The UK Football Association decided to postpone the fifth and sixth rounds of the 1962–63 FA Cup because of delays caused by the severe winter.

7th In the first ballot to select the new leader of Britain's opposition Labour Party, Harold Wilson received 115 votes, George Brown 88, and James Callaghan 41. Since no candidate got a majority of MP votes, a second round would be held on 14th February between Wilson and Brown.

8th Britain's Royal Navy conducted the world's first experimental trials of a vertical take-off and landing fixed-wing aircraft aboard an aircraft carrier, testing the Hawker Siddeley P.1127 prototype aboard HMS Ark Royal.

11th The Beatles recorded the ten songs of their debut album Please Please Me in a single, 13-hour session at the Abbey Road Studios.

14th Harold Wilson was elected leader of Britain's opposition Labour Party, defeating George Brown, Baron George-Brown 144-103 in the second ballot, and putting Wilson in line to be the nation's next Prime Minister when general elections took place.

16th Opinion polls indicate that Labour would defeat the Conservatives at a general election, who have governed since 1951.

18th The Strabane transmitter opens, bringing coverage to the west of Northern Ireland for the first time.

19th Actress Ellis Powell is dismissed from the leading role of Mrs Dale in the BBC Light Programme soap opera The Dales, which she has played since the first episode in 1948, and it is given to former musical actress Jessie Matthews; Powell dies 3 months later aged 57.

March

1st — Eurocontrol, the European Organisation for the Safety of Air Navigation, came into existence as an international treaty signed on 13th December 1960, by West Germany, France, the United Kingdom, Belgium, Netherlands and Luxembourg became effective.

6th — Great Britain's longest, coldest winter in the 20th century started to come to an end, with the ground being snow-free for the first time since the blizzard over the Christmas period. Many places saw their first frost-free night of the year and since before Christmas. The south saw temperatures rose above freezing and into the low 60s Fahrenheit (17 °C).

7th — The first horse race meeting in England since 23rd December 1962 took place, after scheduled races had been called off due to the severe winter conditions.

8th — For the first time in British history, the 25 members of the Scots Guards, personal protectors for Queen Elizabeth II, walked off of their jobs. The grievance, reportedly, was that there was "too much spit and polish".

9th — The Beatles began 1st British tour, supporting Tommy Roe & Chris Montez.

12th — The Beatles perform as a trio, at Granada Cinema, in Bedford, England, as John Lennon is ill with a cold.

14th — In the British courts, Ridge v Baldwin, a landmark case in the law of judicial review, was decided on appeal, holding that a public official cannot be dismissed without first being given notice of the grounds on which the decision was made, as well as an opportunity to be heard in his own defence.

16th — England edges Scotland, 10-8 at Twickenham, London to win its 17th Five Nations Rugby Championship.

The British scientific journal, Nature, published an article by Maarten Schmidt entitled "3C 273: A Star-Like Object with Large Red-Shift", marking the first announcement of the discovery of a quasar (quasi-stellar radio source).

21st — In the UK Parliament, Labour MP George Wigg asked the government to hold hearings on whether Secretary for War John Profumo had behaved inappropriately with missing 20-year-old call girl Christine Keeler.

22nd — The Beatles released their first album, Please Please Me.

27th — Dr. Richard Beeching, the Chairman of British Railways issued the report The Reshaping of British Railways, calling for huge cuts to the United Kingdom's rail network. Over a 12-year period, passenger service would be halted permanently at 29 separate rail routes. An author would note later that 4,500 miles of routes, 2,500 stations, and 67,700 jobs would be ended the closures.

28th — In Wales, Labour Party candidate Neil McBride won the Swansea East by-election caused by the death of Labour Member of Parliament (MP) David Mort.

30th — Graham Hill won the 1963 Lombank Trophy motor race at Snetterton circuit, UK.

April

1st — Engineering Building at the University of Leicester is completed, the first major work by James Stirling with James Gowan, and a leading example of Brutalist architecture.

4th — The Beatles performed at Stowe School in Buckinghamshire, UK, for a fee of £100, having accepted a personal request from schoolboy David Moores, a fellow Liverpudlian (and later chairman of Liverpool F.C.).

5th — The Beatles receive their 1st silver disc (Please Please Me)

9th — Sir Winston Churchill, the former Prime Minister of the United Kingdom, became the first person to be made an honorary citizen of the United States by act of the U.S. Congress, with President Kennedy signing the legislation for the 88-year-old statesman, whose mother had been a United States native. The House of Representatives had approved the legislation on 12th March by a 377–21 vote, and the U.S. Senate approved on 2nd April by voice vote. Churchill was unable to travel from the U.K. to the U.S., and his son, Randolph Churchill, accepted in his place in ceremonies that were televised.

12th — The Beatles third single, "From Me to You" is released in UK.

14th — George Harrison is impressed by unsigned group "Rolling Stones".

15th — Seventy thousand marchers arrived in London from Aldermaston, to demonstrate against nuclear weapons. The breakaway group Spies for Peace set up a picket at RSG-6.

21st — The Beatles meet The Rolling Stones for the 1st time.

24th — Princess Alexandra of Kent marries the Hon. Angus Ogilvy at Westminster Abbey.

May

1st — Sir Winston Churchill announced his retirement from politics at the age of 88, for reasons of health. He pledged that he would remain an M.P. until Parliament was dissolved, but would not stand for re-election.

2nd — The Beatles reach #1 in the UK Singles chart for the first time with "From Me to You".

May

2nd	The Duke of Edinburgh opens the Rootes Group's new car plant at the town of Linwood, Renfrewshire, for the production of its new rear-engine mini-car – the Hillman Imp – to compete against BMC's Mini. It has an economical 875cc engine, and is expected to be developed into luxury Singer and sporty Sunbeam variants in the near future. It is the first new car to be produced in Scotland for thirty years.
7th	The last servicemen are released from conscription as National Service ends.
8th	Dr. No, the first James Bond film, premiered in the United States with Sean Connery as Agent 007. The film had been seen in Europe since its premiere in London on 5th October 1962.
10th	Decca signs Rolling Stones on advice of Beatle George Harrison.
11th	Everton F.C. win the Football League First Division title.
14th	The Rolling Stones signed their first recording contract, after being asked to audition for Decca Records by talent scout Dick Rowe.
15th	The recording of Benjamin Britten's War Requiem wins the composer three Grammy awards. Leslie Bricusse and Anthony Newley win Song of the Year for "What Kind of Fool Am I?"; other nominations include Lionel Bart for "As Long as He Needs Me".
	Tottenham Hotspur become the first British football team to win a European trophy when a 5–1 win over Atlético Madrid in Rotterdam gives them the European Cup Winners' Cup.
24th	Project Emily came to an end in the United Kingdom when the last squadron of Thor nuclear missile stations, at RAF Hemswell, was disbanded.
26th	The 1963 Monaco Grand Prix was won by Graham Hill.
29th	On the 50th anniversary of its stormy première, The Rite of Spring was performed by the London Symphony Orchestra, conducted by 88-year-old Pierre Monteux at the Royal Albert Hall. The composer, 81-year-old Igor Stravinsky, was in the audience as an honoured guest.

June

5th — Profumo affair: John Profumo, Secretary of State for War, admits to misleading Parliament and resigns over his affair with Christine Keeler.

7th — The Rolling Stones' first single, "Come On", was released in the UK, by Decca Records. The cover of "an obscure Chuck Berry ditty" would reach #21 on the British chart.

8th — Profumo affair: Stephen Ward charged with living on immoral earnings.

9th — Jim Clark won the 1963 Belgian Grand Prix.

Spa Francorchamps 14,120 km

12th — "Cleopatra" directed by Joseph Mankiewicz and starring Elizabeth Taylor and Richard Burton premieres in NYC, then most expensive film ever made.

17th — The Profumo affair has done the Conservative government no favours in the opinion polls, which continue to show that a Labour victory would be inevitable at a general election.

20th — The Beatles form "Beatles Ltd" to handle their income.

23rd — Jim Clark won the 1963 Dutch Grand Prix at Zandvoort.

24th — 1st demonstration of home video recorder, at BBC Studios, London.

The Telcan, the first system designed to be used at home for recording programs from a television set, was given its first demonstration. The system, shown in Nottingham, England, was seen to record programs onto a reel of videotape and then to play them back with "very fair video quality" on a 17-inch TV, could hold 30 minutes of programming, and had a suggested retail price of £60 ($175).

26th — Paul McCartney and John Lennon wrote their hit song She Loves You, while staying at the Turk's Hotel in Newcastle-upon-Tyne. Paul would later recall that when he played the recording for his father, the elder McCartney suggested (unsuccessfully) that "yeah, yeah, yeah" should be replaced with "Yes! Yes! Yes!".

July

1st   Kim Philby named as the "Third Man" in the Burgess and Maclean spy ring.

5th   1st Beatles' tune to hit US charts, Del Shannon's cover of "From Me to You" at no. 87.

Wimbledon Men's Tennis: American Chuck McKinley wins his only Grand Slam singles title beating Fred Stolle of Australia 9-7, 6-1, 6-4.

13th   With his popularity declining, British Prime Minister Harold Macmillan fired seven senior members of his cabinet, including Chancellor of the Exchequer Selwyn Lloyd, the Lord Chancellor, the Ministers of Defence and Education, and the Secretary of State for Scotland. The move was unprecedented in United Kingdom history, and was followed by the firing of nine junior ministers on Monday. Liberal MP Jeremy Thorpe would quip, "Greater love hath no man than this that he lay down his friends for his life." The British press would dub the event Macmillan's "Night of the Long Knives".

14th   In the third match of the rugby league Test series between Australia and Great Britain, held at Sydney Cricket Ground, a controversial last-minute Australian try and the subsequent conversion resulted in an 18–17 win for Australia.

20th   The world's first regular passenger hovercraft service was introduced, as the VA-3 began the 20-mile run between Rhyl (in Wales) and Wallasey (in England).

22nd   Please Please Me became the first record album by The Beatles to be released in the United States. Vee Jay Records deleted two of the songs that had appeared on the British version introduced on 22nd March including the title song, "Please Please Me".

29th   West Indies defeated England in the 4th Test (cricket) by 221 runs, at Headingley, Leeds.

31st   The Peerage Act 1963 received royal assent in the United Kingdom, opening membership in the House of Lords to women, and to more than the 16 members of the peerage of Scotland. In addition, the Act allowed a hereditary peer to disclaim his automatic membership among the Lords, which would clear the way for Alec Douglas-Home to become a member of the House of Commons, then Prime Minister.

August

1st — George Harrison and Paul McCartney sang a duet on a Beatles tape recording of the Goffin-King song "Don't Ever Change" for later broadcasting on BBC radio.

3rd — The Beatles performed at The Cavern Club in Liverpool for the 275th, and final time, nearly 18 months after their first appearance on the Club's stage on 9th February 1961.

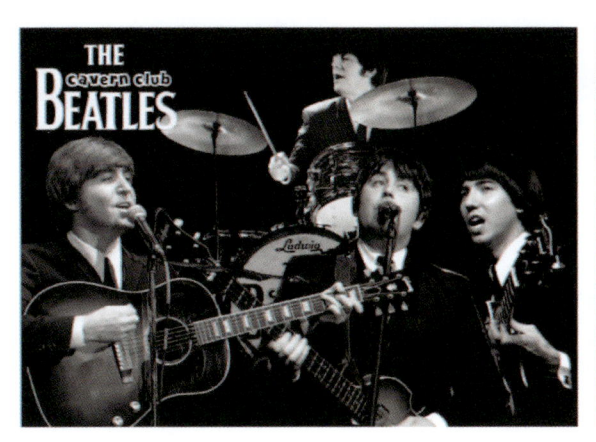

4th — The 1963 German Grand Prix was held at the Nürburgring and won by John Surtees, with Jim Clark finishing second. Clark remained well in first place in the world auto-driving championship standings, with 42 points, while Surtees was second at 22.

5th — The trial of Stephen Ward was formally closed with no sentence pronounced, following Ward's suicide two days earlier.

7th — United Nations Security Council Resolution 181 was passed, calling for a voluntary arms embargo of South Africa because of its racial discrimination. The United States and the United Kingdom abstained from the vote.

8th — The Great Train Robbery of 1963 took place at Ledburn, Buckinghamshire, England, when a gang of bandits halted a train ferrying mail between Glasgow and London. At 3:00 am, the group caused the train's engineer to stop by activating the red signal and covering the green signal. When the train came to a halt, engineer Jack Mills and his assistant were overpowered, while others in the group boarded the first two coaches hauling mail, and tied up the four employees on board. The group then uncoupled the engine and two coaches from the other ten cars on the train, and forced the engineer and assistant to move one mile down the line to the Bridego Bridge, where the mail bags were dropped into automobiles waiting beneath. The haul was estimated at £2,600,000 (at the time worth about $7,300,000; equivalent to $55 million or £37 million in 2013).

9th — The British rock music show Ready Steady Go! premiered on Associated-Rediffusion in London, part of Britain's ITV network, and would later be shown on the other ITV stations. It would run until 7th December 1966.

11th — Jim Clark won the 1963 Kanonloppet motor race at Karlskoga Circuit in Sweden.

14th — British police arrested five persons believed to have been members of the gang that had carried out the robbery of the Glasgow-London mail train the previous week, and recovered £100,000 of the loot that had been stolen.

August

16th   Two people walking in Dorking Woods discovered a briefcase, a holdall and a camel-skin bag, all containing money. The evidence would lead to the arrest of Brian Field, a member of the gang who had carried out the Great Train Robbery a few days earlier. The discovery raised the total amount of money recovered to £141,000 ($394,800).

20th   The Royal Shakespeare Company introduced its performance cycle of Shakespeare's history plays under the title The Wars of the Roses, adapted and directed by John Barton and Peter Hall, at the Royal Shakespeare Theatre, Stratford-upon-Avon.

25th   Paul McCartney is fined 31 pounds & given a 1 yr suspended license for speeding.

26th   West Indies beat England 2-1 in series, 1st holders of Wisden Cricket Trophy.

31st   British North Borneo became the self-governing territory known as Sabah, pending the establishment of the Federation of Malaysia later in the year.

September

1st   The Sindy fashion doll is first marketed by Pedigree. Sindy is a British fashion doll created by Pedigree Dolls & Toys in 1963. A rival to Barbie, Sindy's wholesome look and range of fashions and accessories made her the best-selling toy in the United Kingdom in 1968 and 1970. After Marx Toys' unsuccessful attempt to introduce Sindy in the United States in the late 1970s, Hasbro bought the rights to Sindy and remodelled the doll to look more American. As a result, the doll's popularity declined; in addition, Barbie manufacturer Mattel filed a lawsuit for copyright infringement, which was settled when Hasbro agreed to remodel Sindy's face. During the 1990s, Barbie's share of the doll market continued to grow while Sindy's diminished, which led to Sindy being delisted from major retailers in 1997. Hasbro returned the doll's licence to Pedigree, and the doll was relaunched in 1999, manufactured by Vivid Imaginations. Sindy's 40th anniversary in 2003 saw a new manufacturer, New Moons, and another relaunch and redesign.

5th   British model and showgirl Christine Keeler were arrested for perjury, after witnesses established that she had lied under oath in the criminal trial of Aloysius Gordon in the course of the Profumo affair.

7th   Geophysicists Fred Vine and Drummond Matthews publish proof of seafloor spreading on the Atlantic Ocean floor. Seafloor spreading or Seafloor spread is a process that occurs at mid-ocean ridges, where new oceanic crust is formed through volcanic activity and then gradually moves away from the ridge.

11th   A chartered Vickers 610 Viking airplane, flying from London to Perpignan, France, crashed into the side of the Roc de la Roquette, a mountain in the Pyrenees Range, killing all 40 people on board. All 36 passengers were British tourists Earlier in the day, another Vickers airplane, and Indian Airlines Viscount turboprop, crashed while en route from Nagpur to New Delhi, killing all 18 people on board.

12th   All 36 passengers and four crew of a chartered airliner were killed when the twin-engine VC.1 Viking crashed into a French mountain peak during a thunderstorm. The passengers were all British vacationers who were on their way to the mountain resort town of Perpignan after having departed from London. Shortly after midnight, the aircraft charted from the French company Airnautic, slammed into the 4,800 feet (1,500 m) high Roc de la Rouquette in the French Pyrenees mountains.

September

15th | The Beatles and The Rolling Stones performed in the same show for the first and only time, appearing at a concert at Royal Albert Hall in London.

17th | RAF Fylingdales radar station on the North York Moors begins operation as part of the United States Ballistic Missile Early Warning System. It is a radar base and is also part of the Ballistic Missile Early Warning System (BMEWS). As part of intelligence-sharing arrangements between the United States and United Kingdom (see, for example, the UKUSA Agreement), data collected at RAF Fylingdales are shared between the two countries. Its primary purpose is to give the British and US governments warning of an impending ballistic missile attack (part of the so-called four-minute warning during the Cold War). A secondary role is the detection and tracking of orbiting objects; Fylingdales is part of the United States Space Surveillance Network. As well as its early-warning and space-tracking roles, Fylingdales has a third function – the Satellite Warning Service for the UK. It keeps track of spy satellites used by other countries, so that secret activities in the UK can be carried out when they are not overhead. The armed services, defence manufacturers and research organisations, including universities, take advantage of this facility.

18th | Rioters burn down the British Embassy in Jakarta to protest against the formation of Malaysia.

23rd | The Robbins Report (the report of the Committee on Higher Education, chaired by Lord Robbins) is published. It recommends immediate expansion of universities, and that university places "should be

September

25th — The Denning Report on the Profumo affair is published. The Profumo affair was a major scandal in twentieth-century British politics. John Profumo, the Secretary of State for War in Harold Macmillan's Conservative government, had an extramarital affair with 19-year-old model Christine Keeler beginning in 1961.

26th — Vauxhall launches the new Viva, a small family saloon, similar in size to BMC's 1100 and the Ford Anglia.

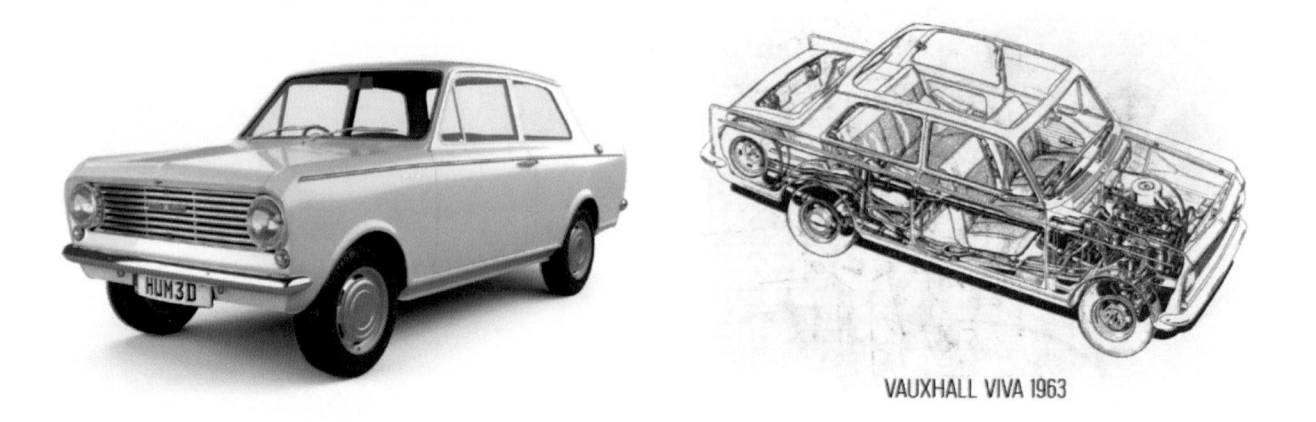

VAUXHALL VIVA 1963

29th — The release of the film Tom Jones. Tom Jones is a 1963 British comedy film, an adaptation of Henry Fielding's classic 1749 novel The History of Tom Jones, a Foundling, starring Albert Finney as the titular hero. It was one of the most critically acclaimed and popular comedies of its time and won four Academy Awards, including Best Picture. The film was produced and directed by Tony Richardson and the screenplay was adapted by playwright John Osborne.

October

2nd — Ford Motor Company begins production of its Ford Anglia car at their new Halewood Body & Assembly plant on Merseyside.

9th — On the first anniversary of its independence from the United Kingdom, Uganda was declared a republic by Prime Minister Milton Obote. The Governor-General, Sir Walter Coutts, stepped down, and the Kabaka (monarch) of Buganda, Sir Edward Mutesa II, became the nation's first President.

10th — In a statement written before he underwent emergency surgery, British Prime Minister Harold Macmillan announced that he would resign on the grounds of ill health, and asked his Conservative Party to select his successor in time for new elections. After his doctors told him that he would be incapacitated until the end of the year, Macmillan made his decision and delivered notes to the Queen and to the Foreign Secretary, Lord Home (Alec Douglas-Home). Lord Home read the surprise announcement at the Conservative Party conference being held at Blackpool.

13th — Four months before they came to the United States, The Beatles performed their latest hit single, "She Loves You" live on the British television variety show Sunday Night at the Palladium. Millions watched on ITV, and the enthusiasm of their fans outside the theatre was so intense that the press later coined the term "Beatlemania".

October

14th — A revolution, called the Aden Emergency by the British press, started in Radfan, South Yemen, against British colonial rule. Backed by the United Arab Republic (Egypt), the rebels were determined to drive the British out of Aden (where they maintained military bases) and the rest of South Yemen (Federation and Protectorate of South Arabia). The last British troops finally withdrew on November 29, 1967.

17th — In Stockholm, two Britons (Alan Lloyd Hodgkin and Andrew Fielding Huxley) and an Australian (John Carew Eccles) were announced as winners of the Nobel Prize in Physiology or Medicine "for their discoveries concerning the ionic mechanisms involved in excitation and inhibition in the peripheral and central portions of the nerve cell membrane".

18th — At 11:00 a.m., Queen Elizabeth II met with Harold Macmillan, who had resigned as Prime Minister of the United Kingdom earlier that morning, to discuss his recommendations for a successor. Macmillan was a patient at the King Edward VII Hospital for Officers, recovering from surgery. Macmillan endorsed Lord Home as the choice most acceptable to the forming of a new government. Macmillan had resigned after having been incorrectly diagnosed with inoperable prostate cancer. He later revealed that he had been hounded from office by a backbench minority, "a band that in the end does not amount to more than 15 or 20 at the most". Far from terminally ill, Macmillan lived for another 23 years, until his death in 1986 at the age of 92.

19th — At 12:56 pm, an announcement was made from Buckingham Palace that the 14th Earl of Home had been formally invited by Queen Elizabeth to succeed Harold Macmillan as the new Prime Minister of the United Kingdom. He was the first member of the nobility since (Robert Gascoyne-Cecil, 3rd Marquess of Salisbury, from 1895 to 1902) to serve as Prime Minister, and "the only man in modern times to do so without a seat in either house of Parliament", having resigned from the House of Lords to run as a candidate for a by-election to the House of Commons. Three of Home's rivals within the Conservative Party, each of whom had aspired to the premiership, agreed to serve in his cabinet. Deputy Prime Minister R.A. "Rab" Butler, Chancellor of the Exchequer Reginald Maudling, and Viscount Hailsham joined Home in order to form a government in advance of the 1964 elections.

21st — The term "Beatlemania" was first used in print, coined for the headline in a feature story for the London tabloid The Daily Mail. The feature story on the group's popularity, written by Vincent Mulchrone, carried the headline "This Beatlemania". On 2nd November another London paper, The Daily Mirror, reported on a concert the night before, in a news story with the headline "BEATLEMANIA! It's happening everywhere... even in sedate Cheltenham".

22nd — The National Theatre of Great Britain staged its first production, presenting Hamlet, starring Peter O'Toole, under the direction of Laurence Olivier. The National Theatre's company did not yet have a building of its own, so William Shakespeare's play was performed at the Royal Victorian Theatre, nicknamed "The Old Vic".

23rd — Before a crowd of more than 100,000 at Wembley Stadium, a friendly soccer match was played to celebrate the centennial of the founding of the Football Association in England. With four minutes left in the game, England defeated a "Rest of the World" team, 2-1, on a goal by Jimmy Greaves of Tottenham Hotspur. The Rest players came from Russia, Brazil, West Germany, Czechoslovakia, France, Scotland, Portugal, Spain, and Yugoslavia.

27th — Jimmy Tarbuck made his first appearance at the London Palladium.

November

4th   The Beatles appeared before the British royal family as "the seventh of nineteen acts" in the annual Royal Variety Performance at the Prince of Wales Theatre in London, and played a set of four songs. After the show, the "Fab Four" were greeted by Queen Elizabeth II, and had conversations with the Queen Mother (Queen Elizabeth II's mother), Princess Margaret and Lord Snowden. The event was taped, and the televised broadcast on November 11 would be watched by what was then a record 26 million viewers.

8th   Sir Alec Douglas-Home, the new Prime Minister of the United Kingdom, won the by-election for Kinross and Western Perthshire, to fill the House of Commons vacancy left by the 15th August death of Gilmour Leburn. Placed as a candidate in one of the most conservative constituencies in the nation, Home drew more than 57% of the vote, with more than twice as much as Liberal Party candidate Alistair Duncan Millar or Labour candidate Andrew Forrester. Having renounced his title and his place in the House of Lords, the former Lord Home became an MP in the House of Commons for the first time.

10th   An American version of the British television news satire That Was the Week That Was was shown at 9:00 p.m. Eastern time as a special broadcast on NBC-TV, and would become a regular series two months later for the pilot, the host was Henry Fonda. Supporting players would include Woody Allen, Steve Allen, Bill Cosby, and future M*A*S*H star Alan Alda.

18th   The Dartford Tunnel under the River Thames opened in the United Kingdom, 164 years after the idea had first been proposed in 1799. The Dartford-Thurrock River Crossing, commonly known as the Dartford Crossing and until 1991 the Dartford Tunnel, is a major road crossing of the River Thames in England, carrying the A282 road between Dartford in Kent in the south and Thurrock in Essex in the north. It consists of two bored tunnels and the cable-stayed Queen Elizabeth II Bridge. The only fixed road crossing of the Thames east of Greater London, it is the busiest estuarial crossing in the United Kingdom, with an average daily use of over 130,000 vehicles. It opened in stages: the west tunnel in 1963, the east tunnel in 1980 and the bridge in 1991. The crossing, although not officially designated a motorway, is considered part of the M25 motorway's route, using the tunnels northbound and bridge southbound. Described as one of the most important road crossings in Britain, it suffers from heavy traffic and congestion.

November

20th | The deathbed wishes of Aldous Huxley, author of Brave New World, was honoured by his wife Laura, who injected him with 200 micrograms of the hallucinogen LSD. The drug was delivered to her by recently fired Harvard University Professor Timothy Leary. Huxley would die two days later.

22nd | C. S. Lewis, the author most famous for the Narnia books (1950–1955), dies aged sixty-five years old in Oxford. However, media coverage of his death (as also that of Aldous Huxley in the United States on the same day) is overshadowed by the assassination of American President John F. Kennedy, news of which reaches the UK just after 18:30 UTC.

23rd | First episode of the BBC Television science fiction series Doctor Who is broadcast with William Hartnell as the First Doctor. The series runs until 1989 and is revived from 2005.

25th | The Duke of Edinburgh, Prime Minister Sir Alec Douglas-Home and Leader of the Opposition Harold Wilson attend the funeral of U.S. President John F. Kennedy in Washington, D.C.

30th | After an unbroken 30-week spell at the top of the UK Albums Chart, The Beatles album Please Please Me is knocked off the top of the charts by the group's latest album With the Beatles (released on 22nd November).

December

7th | Americans got their first glimpse of the new British music group, The Beatles, when a clip of one of their performances (and the enthusiastic support from the British fans) was shown on the CBS Evening News. Radio stations in the U.S. began receiving requests to play Beatles songs, and several began to import copies from the U.K.

12th | The Beatles reach No. 1 for the third time (according to the 'official' chart) with the Lennon–McCartney single "I Want to Hold Your Hand" (released on 29 November).

13th | The Beatles made the last of their 34 appearances on their autumn tour of the UK and Ireland, wrapping up at the Gaumont Cinema in Southampton, before breaking for Christmas.

December

21st "The Daleks", a serial that marked the fifth episode of the Doctor Who science fiction television series, saw the introduction of the Dalek robots, the most famous of all the nemeses in the program's history. In the episode "The Dead Planet", Doctor Who and his three companions arrived in the TARDIS on the planet Skaro, although viewers would not see what a Dalek looked like until the December 28 show.

26th The United Kingdom, Greece and Turkey created the Joint Truce Force to enforce a ceasefire in Cyprus.

28th The satirical BBC show That Was the Week That Was (TW3) airs for the last time.

30th The pilot edition of I'm Sorry, I'll Read That Again was broadcast on the BBC Home Service under the title Cambridge Circus.

ADVERTS OF 1963

BSA Motorcycles for 1963

Destination *Fun!*

**NEW MODELS
NEW FEATURES**

**THE NEW GOLD STAR TWIN
—Plus 14 other sparkling models**

2 ADDITIONAL "COMMERCIALS" FOR YOUR DINKY FLEET

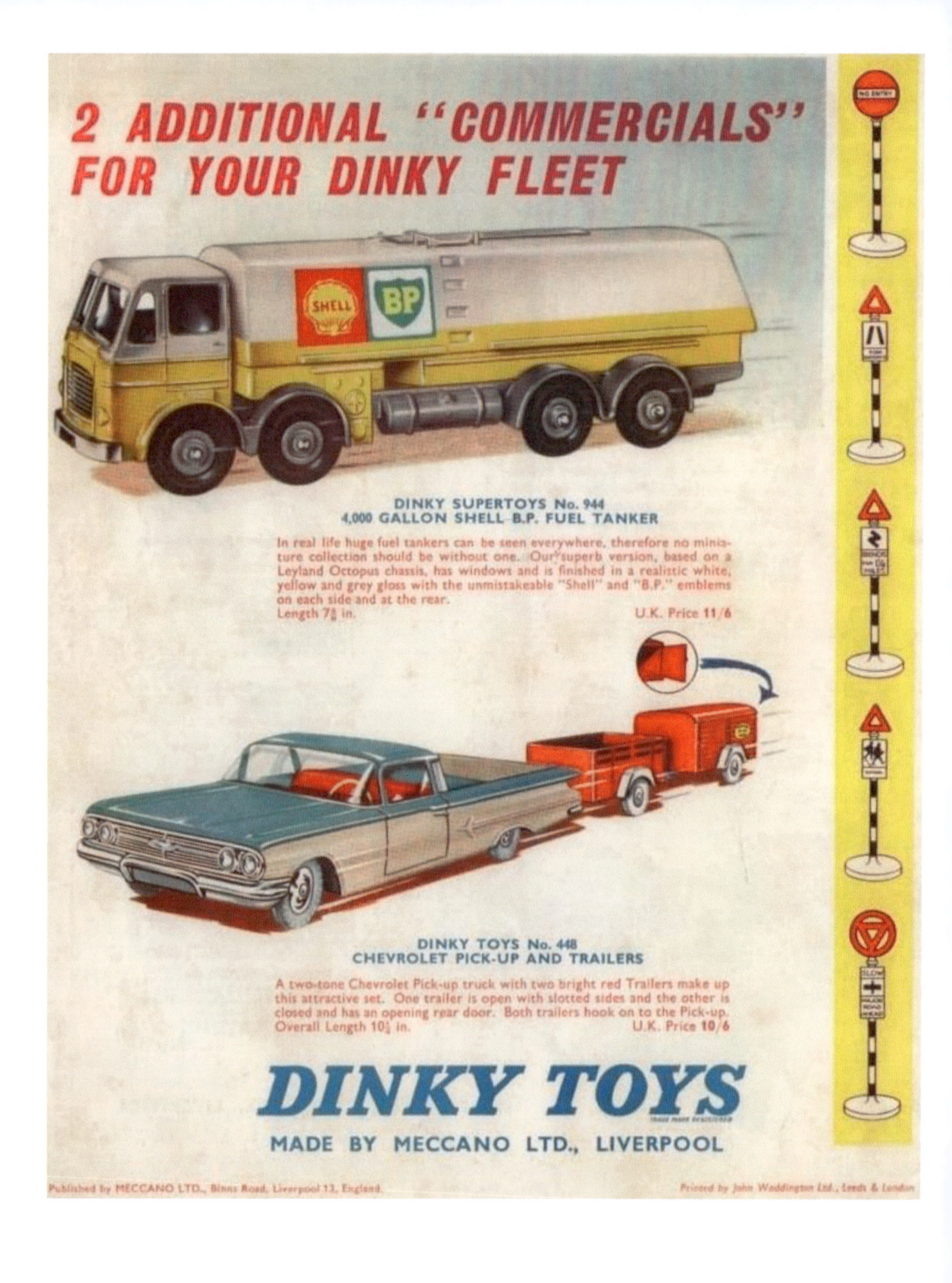

DINKY SUPERTOYS No. 944
4,000 GALLON SHELL B.P. FUEL TANKER

In real life huge fuel tankers can be seen everywhere, therefore no miniature collection should be without one. Our superb version, based on a Leyland Octopus chassis, has windows and is finished in a realistic white, yellow and grey gloss with the unmistakeable "Shell" and "B.P." emblems on each side and at the rear.
Length 7⅜ in. U.K. Price 11/6

DINKY TOYS No. 448
CHEVROLET PICK-UP AND TRAILERS

A two-tone Chevrolet Pick-up truck with two bright red Trailers make up this attractive set. One trailer is open with slotted sides and the other is closed and has an opening rear door. Both trailers hook on to the Pick-up.
Overall Length 10½ in. U.K. Price 10/6

DINKY TOYS
MADE BY MECCANO LTD., LIVERPOOL

Published by MECCANO LTD., Binns Road, Liverpool 13, England. Printed by John Waddington Ltd., Leeds & London

Holidays abroad by motor coach
DINKY TOYS No. 953—CONTINENTAL TOURING COACH
Paris, Rome, Brussels, Vienna . . . all these cities, and many more, are visited every year by hundreds of coaches similar to the prototype of this Dinky Supertoy. The model itself is fitted with specially tinted windows, seats and steering wheel and is finished in a delightful pale blue gloss with white roof. The words "Dinky Continental Tours" appear on each side.
U.K. Price 13/6
The last word in realism!
DINKY TOYS No. 277
SUPERIOR CRITERION AMBULANCE WITH FLASHING LIGHT
With siren wailing and roof-light flashing the ambulance rushes its patient to hospital! This striking miniature also is fitted with a red roof-light which actually flashes as the vehicle is pushed along. Realistic figures of driver and attendant occupy the front seats. These refinements are additional to the regular Dinky Toys features—Prestomatic steering, windows, suspension and seats.
Length 5 in.
U.K. Price 8/9
Battery No. 036 (Vidor V16) is not supplied with the model, but may be purchased separately. Price 5d.
DINKY TOYS
MADE BY MECCANO LTD.
AVAILABLE LATER OVERSEAS
Printed by John Waddington Ltd., Leeds & London

Kind hearts give CORONETS...
and DUKES...and CROWNS
DONCELLA
Cigars
CROWNS
SMALL CORONA
FOUR
Player's have made it easy to give the right cigars for Christmas. There are now three sizes of Doncellas—Coronets, Dukes and Crowns.
All are mild and mellow blends of Havana and other fine tobaccos, firmly rolled, and individually wrapped and sealed in perfect condition . . . the qualities every cigar-smoker looks for. They are specially rolled in London for John Player and Sons and guaranteed by them.
Coronets - five for 3/11½
Dukes - four for 5/6
Crowns - four for 8/4
DONCELLA CIGARS

New Triumph Spitfire—12 feet long, every inch a sports car.
goes over 90 m.p.h., independent suspension on all 4 wheels.
Triumph engineering all the way. You own it for only $2199:
DESIGN: Four cylinder engine. Dual carburetors. Four speed gear box. Independent suspension on all wheels. Disc brakes. Racing hand brake.
STYLING: Body created by the noted Italian designer Michelotti. (Look at those pictures again.) Roll-up windows. Lockable doors and trunk. Easily erected, all weather top. Leather grained upholstery. Full-scale, competition tested instrument panel including tachometer.
PERFORMANCE: Top speed over 90. Accelerates 0-60 m.p.h. in 16.5 seconds, 30-50 m.p.h. (traffic passing range) in 7 seconds. Up to 35 miles per gallon (over 300 miles without refueling). Turning circle only 24 feet.
TEST DRIVE a real live Spitfire at your Triumph dealer's. (He's in the Yellow Pages.) Compare the ride with any car in the class. Compare features. Then compare the $2199 price! Discover a new standard of sports-car value.
Triumph Spitfire

GET AROUND BETTER-TRAVEL...
835 DYW
Lambretta!
Say goodbye . . . to queues, traffic jams and parking problems and enjoy the carefree independence that only a Lambretta can provide. For your daily journey, weekend pleasure or the holiday of your life, Lambretta scooters provide the most efficient, economical form of mechanical transport yet devised. Superbly styled, thoroughly tested, incredibly reliable, clean to ride, easy to handle, capable of cruising at 50 mph and costing well under 1d. a mile for fuel, Lambretta Scooters are available in a wide range of eye-catching colours from a network of appointed Dealers that extends throughout the United Kingdom. All Lambretta Dealers are equipped to provide YOU with efficient Sales, Service and Spares facilities, to take your present model in part-exchange, to quote hire purchase terms that are unsurpassed and to arrange cover under the Lambretta Insurance Scheme at the highly preferential rates that apply as a result of Lambretta's excellent safety record.
all this from £30 down!
SEE US ON STAND No. 12
BLACKPOOL CYCLE SHOW
and 36 monthly payments of £4·9·8
(Less than 25/- per week)
Lambretta 125 Cash price £148·1·1 (inc. Pillion Seat)
To: Lambretta Concessionaires Limited
Trojan Works · Purley Way · Croydon
Please send me literature on Lambretta scooters
NAME
ADDRESS
SEND OFF THIS COUPON TODAY!

No wonder you women buy more TIDE than any other washday product!
TIDE'S GOT WHAT WOMEN WANT!
NO SOAP-NO OTHER "SUDS"-NO OTHER WASHING PRODUCT KNOWN-WILL GET YOUR WASH AS CLEAN AS TIDE!
New washing miracle
Tide
ONLY TIDE DOES ALL THREE:
1. World's CLEANEST wash!
2. World's WHITEST wash!
3. Actually BRIGHTENS colors!
TIDE'S A SUDSING WHIZZ EVEN IN HARDEST WATER
THERE'S NOTHING LIKE PROCTER & GAMBLE'S TIDE
REMEMBER!
TIDE GETS CLOTHES CLEANER THAN ANY OTHER WASHDAY PRODUCT YOU CAN BUY!

CERTINA
automatic
blue ribbon
27
Make the most of
CERTINA
watches
1963 stretches ahead. It should be a good year for you! As a Certina stockist you should be in for a boom time. Because Certina watches are doing better than ever before. The figures prove it: sales are ripping, all over the country. So make the most of these invaluable money-spinners. You've got a superb product to sell—so stock it. You've got free dealer blocks any time you like to ask for them (6" D.C. size)—so ask for them. And any time you want our illustrated catalogue showing the exciting new models, just let us know.
MAKE 1963 YOUR BOOM YEAR!
Carley & Clemence Limited, 49 Hatton Garden, London, E.C.1. Tel: Holborn 3345

a Dormobile day is fun -all the way
DORMOBILE
Settle family and friends into those six comfortable seats with their wide-view windows. Enjoy every minute of your touring. Time for refreshment? There's that neat cooker for a quick cup of tea or a full meal. And at the end of the day, choose your stopping place and enjoy all the comforts of your own holiday chalet-on-wheels. The patent "Dormatic" seating instantly converts to 2 full-length beds, you have built-in sink unit with water supply, dining facilities, cupboard and wardrobe space—and on 4-berth models, that high elevating roof with its 2 extra berths. And remember . . . holidays over, a Dormobile is just as handy for everyday transport.
Illustrated is the 6-seater 4-berth Dormobile caravan conversion of the Thames 10/12 cwt. van £826/10/- (no. P.T.). 2-berth models from £707/10/- (no P.T.).
Dormobile caravan conversions of Bedford, Austin J4, Morris J4, Commer ½ ton, long wheelbase Land-Rover and Volkswagen vans also available.
All are Martin Walter quality products.
DORMOBILE
TRADE MARK
CARAVAN
WORLD'S LARGEST PRODUCERS OF MOTORISED CARAVANS
Ask your dealer for a demonstration, or post coupon for illustrated catalogue to the designers and builders.
Martin Walter Ltd
Dormobile Works, Folkestone. Telephone: Folkestone 51844. Est. 1773.
VISIT US AT THE MOTOR SHOW, EARLS COURT, STAND 142
To: MARTIN WALTER, Ltd. Dormobile Works, Folkestone, Kent
Please send me illustrated catalogue of Thames DORMOBILE Caravan and name of my nearest dealer.
NAME
ADDRESS
(BLOCK CAPITALS PLEASE)

Cherries and Brandy
Tradition and Care
Very Cheering Cherry Heering
in a nutshell...
The finest
CHERRY BRANDY
is
CHERRY HEERING
CHERRY HEERING
CHERRY BRANDY
Have you a bottle in the house?

FOCUS ON FLAVOR
Winston
FILTER CIGARETTES
FINER FILTER FOR FINER FLAVOR
Get the full picture on smoking enjoyment.
Try the one cigarette that has a pure white, modern filter
plus all the flavor of Filter-Blend up front—Winston!
PURE WHITE, MODERN FILTER
PLUS FILTER-BLEND UP FRONT
Winston tastes good
like a cigarette should!

24

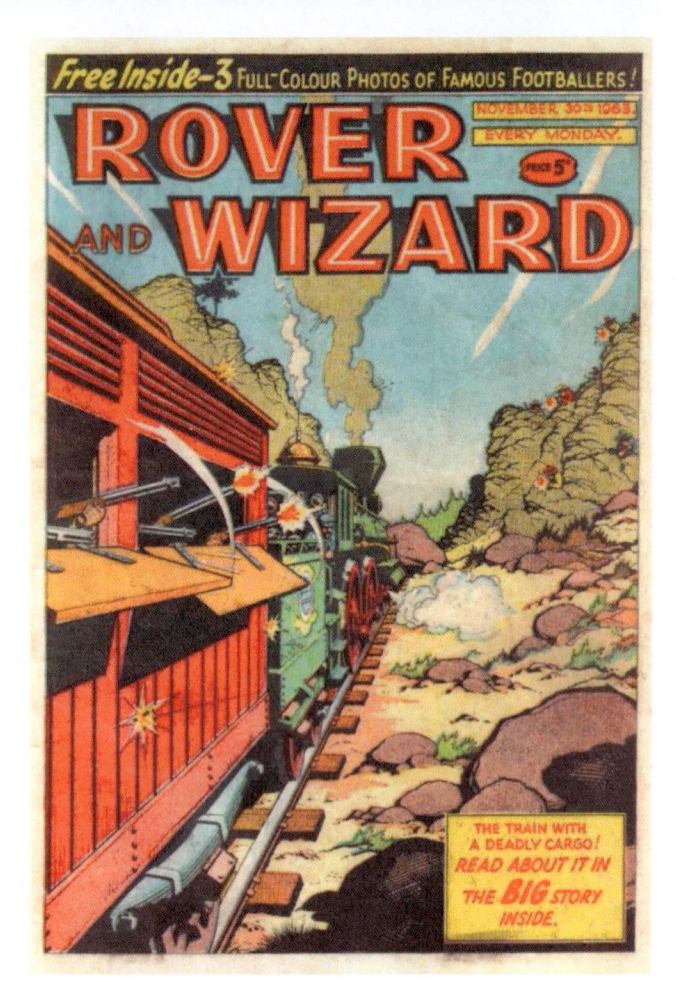

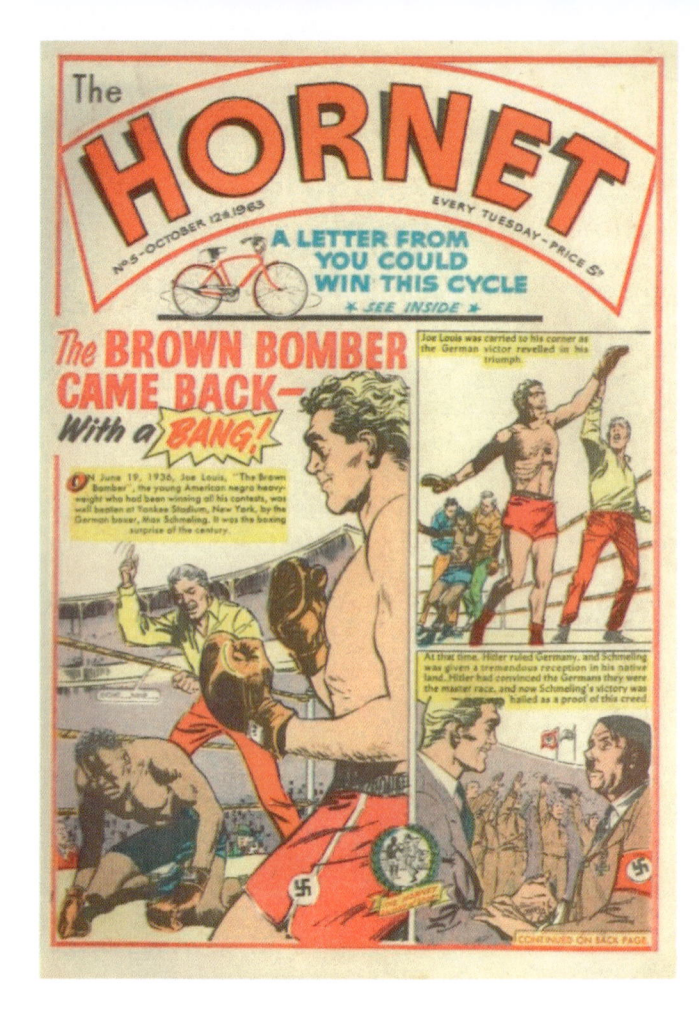

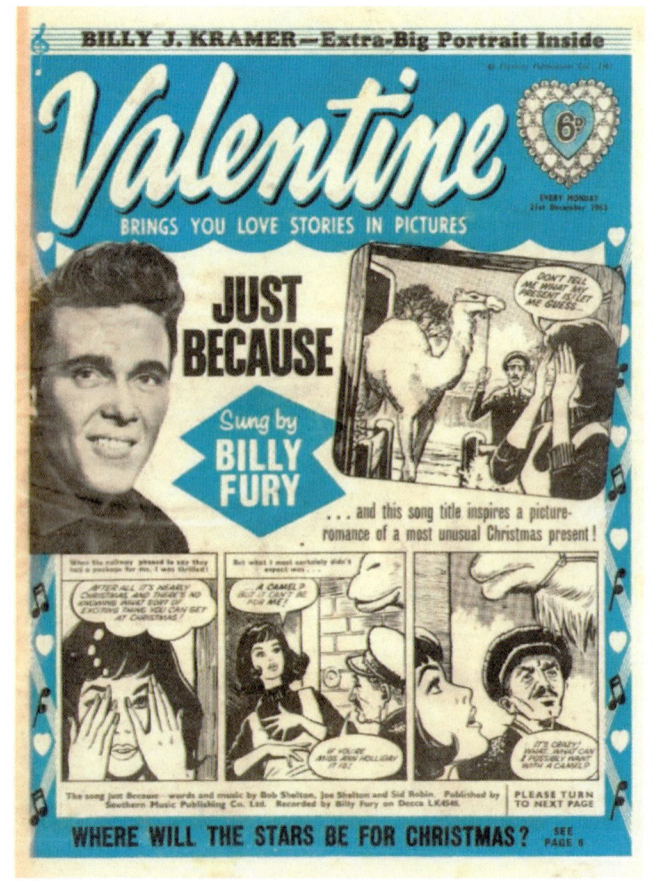

GOOD FOR YOU

"I should like to send you this appreciation of the value of Guinness as a drink and a food. After a hard day's work in my medical practice, I have established the habit of taking a Guinness as an aperitif before my dinner, and usually enjoy a second glass with my meal. It has proved an excellent fortification in this dismal winter weather." M.B., B.S., F.R.C.S., L.R.C.P.

The Doctor who wrote this letter has given us special permission to publish it.

The Doctor who wrote this letter has given us special permission to publish it.

COST OF LIVING 1963

A conversion of pre-decimal to decimal money

The Pound, 1971 became the year of decimalization when the pound became 100 new pennies. Prior to that the pound was equivalent to 20 shillings. Money prior to 1971 was written £/s/d. (d being for pence). Below is a chart explaining the monetary value of each coin before and after 1971.

Symbol	Before 1971	After 1971
£	Pound (240 pennies)	Pound (100 new pennies)
s	Shilling (12 pennies)	5 pence
d	Penny	¼ of a penny
¼d	Farthing	1 penny
½d	Halfpenny	½ pence
3d	Threepence	About 1/80 of a pound
4d	Groat (four pennies)	
6d	Sixpence (Tanner)	2½ new pence
2s	Florin (2 shillings)	10 pence
2s/6d	Half a crown (2 shillings and 6 pence)	12½ pence
5s	Crown	25 pence
10s	10-shilling note (10 bob)	50 pence
10s/6d	½ Guinea	52½ pence
21s	1 Guinea	105 pence

Prices are in equivalent to new pence today and on average throughout the UK.

Item	1963	Price equivalent today
Wages, average yearly	£633.00	£12,729.00
Average house price	£2,880.00	£43,295.00
Price of an average car	£675.00	£9,482.00
Gallon of petrol	5s 9d	£1.08p
Pepsi Cola (3 cans)	2s 6d	£1.90p
Maxwell House Coffee	4s 11d for 4oz	£3.85p
Skyline 67 tin opener	1s 10d	£1.40p
Milk 1 pint	8½d	£0.54p
Stork Butter ½lb	1s 9d	£1.32p
1 cwt of coal delivered	8s -12s	£6 - £9
Dansette Conquest Auto record player	£23 19s 6d	£360.00
The Daily Mirror newspaper	3d	19p
Beer (Pint)	2s 1d	£1.60p
20 Cigarettes	4s 6d	£3.40p

Man's nylon shirt (Woolworths) - 19s 11d
Women's permanently pleated skirt (Woolworths) - 19s 11d
Air bed (Woolworths) - 19s 6d
22" suitcase (Woolworths) - 19s 6d
Polythene coal hod (Woolworths) - 19s 6d
24" electric fire (Woolworths) - 19s
Folding stool (Woolworths) - 18s 6d
Parker Jotter ballpoint pen - 20s
Chocolate Tobler Toblerone 6d, 1/3, or 1/9
Mackintosh Quality Street 1lb - 5/10

Stresco Hiker's Stove (portable petrol stove) - 19s 6d
COIL S 372 battery slide viewer - 18s
Dubonnet aperitif wine (bottle) - 18s 6d
Dewar's White Label whisky (half bottle) - 19s 6d
Artificial suntan (bottle) - 17s 6d
Helix Everest school geometry set - 19s 9d
Child's duffle coat (J A Davis) - 19s
Pifco Flashing Lantern (Halfords) - 18s 11d
Duffle bag (Halfords) - 19s 6d
Cycle touring bag (Halfords) - 19s
Sutty Cyclone Mk1 foot pump for car - (Halfords) - 19s 6d
Reconditioned Army boots (pair) - 19s 6d

Cadbury's Milk Tray (launched 1915) - 1lb 7/6 (*)
Cadbury's Continental - 1lb 15/-
Cadbury's Roses - 1lb 6/-
Cadbury's Contrast - 1lb 8/3
Chocolate Tobler Ballerina assortment (milk) 1lb - 8/9
Chocolate Tobler Symphony assortment (plain) 1lb - 9/-
Mackintosh Good News 1lb - 8/-
Mackintosh Week End Assortment 1lb - 7/6
Mackintosh Reward Assortment 1lb - 7/-
Nestle's Home Made Assortment 1lb - 9/-
Nestle's Soft Centres 1lb - 7/3
Nestle's Cailler Frigor 1lb - 5/9
Rowntree's Black Magic 1lb - 8/3
Rowntree's Dairy Box 1lb - 7/6
Terry's All Gold 1lb - 10/-

19" Philips dual standard black & white TV (Currys)	69 guineas	£1,100
Frigidaire SheerLook refrigerator	£39	£590
Murphy-Richards TOS toaster	£5 18s 6d	£90
Hoover Constellation 862 vacuum cleaner	£19 12s 6d	£300
Dent-o-matic electric tooth brush	£4 4s	£64

Coffee Brands from the 60's

Tea was still Britain's favourite drink in the 60s and Britons consumed more tea per head than any other nationality. However, tea was going out of favour. More and more people were putting on the kettle to make a cup of instant coffee instead. Coffee brought a touch of continental sophistication to the UK. The generation gap spread to the choice of coffee or tea. Older people still preferred Britain's traditional cuppa, but by the end of the sixties, young housewives were stocking up with jars of instant coffee from Tesco, Sainsbury or Fine Fare instead.

Express Aroma Rich	**4s 4d for 4oz**
Lyons	3s 9d for 4oz
Nescafé	**4s 11d for 4oz**
Nescafé Gold Blend	6s for 4oz
Nescafé Blend 37	**6s 4d for 4oz**
Summer Gold (United Dairies)	4s 3d for 4oz
Kenco Mild Roast	**5s 6d for 4oz**
Kenco Continental High Roast	3s 3d for 2oz

Kodak Automatic cine camera	**£24 10s 2d**	**£370**
Servis Supertwin - washing machine (Currys)	77 guineas	£1,200
Lec F160 chest freezer	**£103 9s 7d**	**£1,600**
Rolls-Colston Mk IV dishwasher	£78 15s	£1,200
Axminster carpet per square yard	**82s**	**£62**
Russell Hobbs K2 electric kettle	£5 5s	£80
Aristoc Run Resist No. 1 nylon stockings 15 Denier	**8s 11d**	**£6.80**
Coin operated dry cleaning (Bendix) per load	10s	£7.50

Dansette is one of the most collectable 1960s record players. Restored sets in top condition can sell for up to £500. But you can still pick up reasonable sets, some in working order and good cosmetic condition, for less than £100. As with all electrical items, you must have it checked by a qualified electrician before using.

Dansettes were not the design establishment's favourite though. The design awards went to Murphy and Bush. Dansettes were more about fun and fashion than good design.

The Rank Organisation bought the name and continued to make record players branded Dansette in the early 1970s.

BRITISH BIRTHS

Jason Joseph Connery was born 11th January 1963 and is a British actor and director. He is the son of Sean Connery and Diane Cilento. On screen, he is best known for appearing in the third series of the ITV drama series Robin of Sherwood in 1986. He took over the main role after Michael Praed's character was killed off at the end of the second series. His film début was in The Lords of Discipline (1983). He appeared in the Doctor Who serial Vengeance on Varos in 1985; he also portrayed Robin Hood in the final series of the television series Robin of Sherwood in 1986. He later portrayed James Bond creator Ian Fleming in the 1990 television drama Spy maker: The Secret Life of Ian Fleming. In 1997, he appeared in a fantasy film playing the title role of Merlin in Merlin: The Quest Begins. In 2008, he made his directorial début with the film Pandemic and in 2009 directed The Devil's Tomb. In 2016, Connery directed Tommy's Honour, a film celebrating the lives of golf pioneers Old Tom Morris and Young Tom Morris.

James Daniel May was born 16th January 1963 and is an English television presenter and journalist. He is best known as a co-presenter of the motoring programme Top Gear alongside Jeremy Clarkson and Richard Hammond from 2003 until 2015. He also served as a director of the production company W. Chump & Sons, which has since ceased operating. He is a co-presenter of the television series The Grand Tour for Amazon Prime Video, alongside his former Top Gear colleagues, Clarkson and Hammond, as well as Top Gear's former producer Andy Wilman. During the early 1980s, May worked as a sub-editor for The Engineer and later Autocar magazine, from which he was dismissed for performing a prank. May was briefly a co-presenter of the original Top Gear series during 1999. He first co-presented the revived series of Top Gear in its second series in 2003 where he earned the nickname "Captain Slow" owing to his careful driving style.

John Simon Bercow was born 19th January 1963 is a British politician who was Speaker of the House of Commons from 2009 to 2019, and Member of Parliament (MP) for Buckingham between 1997 and 2019. A member of the Conservative Party prior to becoming Speaker, he was the first MP since Selwyn Lloyd in 1971 to be elected Speaker without having been a Deputy Speaker. After resigning as Speaker in 2019 and opting not to seek re-election as MP for Buckingham in the 2019 general election, Bercow left Parliament. In 2021 he joined the Labour Party. On the resignation of Michael Martin in June 2009, Bercow stood successfully in the election to replace him as Speaker. As Speaker, he was obliged to leave the Conservative Party and remain as an independent for the duration of his tenure. He was re-elected unopposed at the commencements of the Parliaments in 2010, 2015 and 2017. This made him the first Speaker since the Second World War to have been elected four times.

Andrew John Ridgeley was born 26th January 1963 is an English singer, songwriter, and record producer, best known for his work in the 1980s in the musical duo Wham! After years of playing in various music groups, most notably The Executive, Michael and Ridgeley formed the duo Wham! in 1981. Michael was lead vocalist and primary songwriter, and played keyboards, while Ridgeley played guitar and performed backing vocals. They approached various record labels with a homemade demo tape—which took 10 minutes to record in Ridgeley's living room—and signed with Innervision Records (distributed by CBS Records). After one album, the duo signed with Epic Records/CBS. In 1984, Wham! charted two U.K. No. 1 singles, and were competing that year with pop rivals Duran Duran to be Britain's biggest pop act. Upon hearing of Michael's death on 25 December 2016, Ridgeley paid his respects on Twitter, saying, "Heartbroken at the loss of my beloved friend Yog."

Stephen Vincent McGann was born 2nd February 1963 is a British actor, author, and science communicator, best known for portraying Doctor Patrick Turner in the BBC One medical period drama series Call the Midwife. He is one of a family of acting brothers including Joe, Paul, and Mark. In 1989, he starred as Mickey in the West End hit musical Blood Brothers. In 1990, he played Johann Strauss in the international mini-series, The Strauss Dynasty. In 1993, he created, co-produced and starred in the award-winning BBC drama The Hanging Gale. He portrayed the character of Sean Reynolds in Emmerdale from 1999 to 2002. In 2003, he starred with Jamie Theakston in the hit West End play 'Art'. In 2006, he played the role of the Reverend Shaw in the original West End cast of the musical Footloose. He can currently be seen playing Dr. Turner in BBC TV series Call the Midwife. In addition to his acting, McGann is a public speaker and communicator of science.

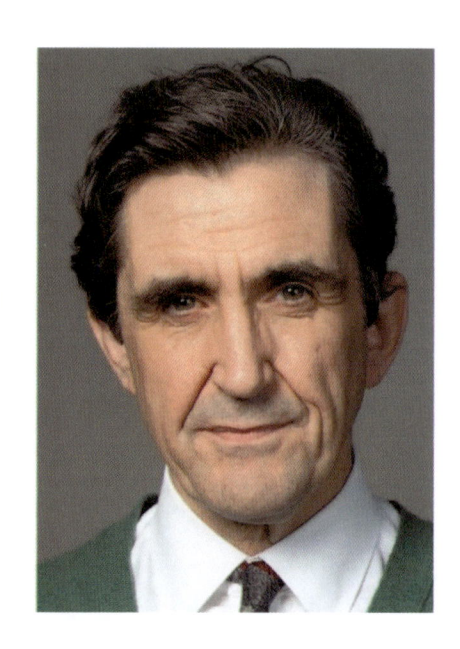

Philip Haywood Glenister born 10th February 1963 is an English actor. In the early 1990s, Glenister appeared in various TV series including Minder, The Ruth Rendell Mysteries, Heartbeat, The Chief, Dressing for Breakfast and Silent Witness. In 1997, he appeared in Sharpe's Justice as Richard Sharpe's half-brother Matt Truman. In 2001, he appeared in two of the Hornblower TV films as Horatio's antagonist Gunner Hobbs. Glenister played the photographer who took nude photos for a Women's Institute fundraising calendar in the 2003 feature film Calendar Girls. Glenister is probably best known for his role as DCI Gene Hunt in Life on Mars co-starring with John Simm as Sam Tyler, and its sequel Ashes to Ashes with Keeley Hawes as Alex Drake. Glenister also worked with Simm on State of Play and Clocking Off and the 2008 crime film Tuesday. Upon announcement of the film, Glenister joked that he and Simm were contractually obliged to work with each other once a year. In 2011, Glenister reunited with John Simm once more in the Sky TV mini-series Mad Dogs.

Jerome Patrick Flynn was born 16th March 1963 and is an English actor and singer. He is best known for his roles as Paddy Garvey of the King's Fusiliers in the ITV series Soldier Soldier, Fireman Kenny 'Rambo' Baines in the pilot of London's Burning, Bronn in the hit HBO series Game of Thrones, and Bennet Drake in Ripper Street. He and his Soldier Soldier co-star Robson Green also performed as Robson & Jerome in the latter half of the 1990s. They released a version of "Unchained Melody", which stayed at number 1 for 7 weeks on the UK Chart, selling more than a million copies and becoming the best-selling single of 1995. The duo had two further number 1 singles: "I Believe" and "What Becomes of the Broken-hearted". Their eponymous debut album and the follow-up Take Two both reached number 1 on the UK Albums Chart. In 2019, in an interview, Flynn revealed that he'd been cast in Amazon Prime Video's upcoming series adaptation of Stephen King's The Dark Tower series in an unannounced role.

Sean Lock was born 22 April 1963 and sadly passed away on 16th August 2021 and was an English comedian and actor. He began his comedy career as a comedian and in 2000 won the British Comedy Award, in the category of Best Live Comic, and was nominated for the Perrier Comedy Award. Lock's early television work included a supporting role alongside Rob Newman and David Baddiel in the 1993 series Newman and Baddiel in Pieces including touring with them as their support act. In December 1998, he launched his own show on BBC Radio 4, 15 Minutes of Misery originally as a five-episode pilot. In 2005 he became a regular team captain on the Channel 4 panel game 8 Out of 10 Cats. Lock was a supporter of Chelsea F.C. and was an active supporter of the Muswell Hill soup kitchen. On 16th August 2021 Lock died of cancer at his home, aged 58. According to Bill Bailey, a close friend of Lock's, he had been diagnosed with "advanced" lung cancer "a few years ago".

Jason Isaacs was born 6 June 1963 and is an English actor. After successfully completing his training as an actor, Isaacs almost immediately began appearing on the stage and on television; his film debut was in a minor role as a doctor in Mel Smith's The Tall Guy (1989). After appearing in Dragonheart (1996), Isaacs landed his first major Hollywood feature-film role alongside Laurence Fishburne in the horror film Event Horizon (1997) where he played the role of D.J. the Medical Doctor of Lewis and Clark. Isaacs played Major Briggs, an American military officer, opposite Matt Damon and Greg Kinnear, in Paul Greengrass's thriller Green Zone (2010). It was announced in March 2017 that Isaacs would play the role of Captain Gabriel Lorca in the new CBS All Access (or Paramount+) series Star Trek: Discovery. In November 2019, it was announced that Isaacs will appear beside Jim Broadbent in the film The Dead Spit of Kelly. Isaacs is involved with a number of charities and in July 2020, announced that he had become patron of the Veterans charity Bravehound.

Colin Stuart Montgomerie, OBE born 23rd June 1963 is a Scottish professional golfer. He has won a record eight European Tour Order of Merit titles, including a streak of seven consecutively from 1993 to 1999. He has won 31 European Tour events, the most of any British player, placing him fourth on the all-time list of golfers with most European Tour victories. Montgomerie won three consecutive Volvo PGA Championships at Wentworth Club between 1998 and 2000. He has finished runner-up on five occasions in major championships and his career-high world ranking is second. He was inducted into the World Golf Hall of Fame in 2013. In June 2013, after turning 50, Montgomerie joined the Champions Tour, where he made his debut in the Constellation Senior Players Championship, one of the five senior major championships. On 25th May 2014, Montgomerie won his first senior major championship at the Senior PGA Championship.

George Michael born Georgios Kyriacos Panayiotou on 25th June 1963 and passed away on the 25th December 2016 and was an English singer, songwriter, and record producer. Michael's first solo single, "Careless Whisper", reached number one in over 20 countries, including the UK and US. Michael's debut solo album, Faith, was released in 1987, topping the UK Albums Chart and staying at number one on the Billboard 200 for 12 weeks. Globally it sold 25 million copies, and four singles from the album—"Faith", "Father Figure", "One More Try", and "Monkey"—reached number one on the Billboard Hot 100. Michael came out as gay in 1998. He was an active LGBT rights campaigner and HIV/AIDS charity fundraiser. Michael is one of the best-selling music artists of all time, with sales of over 120 million records worldwide. In the early hours of 25 December 2016, Michael died in bed at his home in Goring-on-Thames, at the age of 53. A senior coroner in Oxfordshire attributed Michael's death to dilated cardiomyopathy with myocarditis and a fatty liver.

Tracey Karima Emin, CBE, RA was born 3rd July 1963 and is a British artist known for her autobiographical and confessional artwork. Emin produces work in a variety of media including drawing, painting, sculpture, film, photography, neon text and sewn appliqué. Once the "enfant terrible" of the Young British Artists in the 1980s, Tracey Emin is now a Royal Academician. In 1999, Emin had her first solo exhibition in the United States at Lehmann Maupin Gallery, entitled Every Part of Me's Bleeding. Later that year, she was a Turner Prize nominee and exhibited My Bed – a readymade installation, consisting of her own unmade dirty bed, in which she had spent several weeks drinking, smoking, eating, sleeping and having sexual intercourse while undergoing a period of severe emotional flux. Emin was a mentor on the BA Great Britons Programme. She also produced a poster and limited edition print for the London 2012 Olympic and Paralympic Games, one of only 12 British artists selected. In December 2020, Emin had a gallery exhibition containing works by Edvard Munch.

Graham Poll born 29th July 1963 and was an English former football referee in the Premier League. With 26 years of experience, he was one of the most prominent referees in English football, often taking charge of the highest-profile games. His final domestic game in a career spanning 1,544 matches was the Championship play-off final on 28th May 2007 between Derby County and West Bromwich Albion. He was the English representative at two World Cups and UEFA Euro 2000, and refereed the 2005 UEFA Cup Final. In his third game of the 2006 FIFA World Cup in Germany, Croatia vs Australia, he cautioned Croatian defender Josip Šimunić three times before sending him off. Poll retired from refereeing international tournament finals matches shortly afterwards, citing his error in the match. He continued to referee in the Premier League, Champions League and on international games, but said he would not allow himself to be nominated to represent the FA at any tournament finals as he felt he had his chance.

Ian Edward Wright MBE born 3rd November 1963 and is an English former professional footballer, and television and radio personality. He is currently a pundit for BBC Sport and ITV Sport. Ian Wright enjoyed success with London clubs Crystal Palace and Arsenal as a forward, spending six years with the former and seven years with the latter. With Arsenal he lifted the Premier League title, both the major domestic cup competitions, and the European Cup Winners Cup. Known for his speed, agility, finishing and aggression. He played 581 league games, scoring 287 goals for seven clubs in Scotland and England, while also earning 33 caps for the England national team, and scoring nine international goals. Wright also played in the Premier League for West Ham United, the Scottish Premier League for Celtic and the Football League for Burnley and Nottingham Forest. As of 2021, he is Arsenal's second-highest scorer of all time and Crystal Palace's third-highest. After retiring, he has been active in the media, usually in football-related TV and radio shows.

Hugh Richard Bonneville Williams DL was born 10th November 1963 is an English actor. He is best known for playing Robert Crawley, Earl of Grantham in the ITV historical drama series Downton Abbey. Bonneville's first professional stage appearance was at the Open-Air Theatre, Regent's Park. In 1987, he joined the National Theatre where he appeared in several plays, then the Royal Shakespeare Company in 1991, where he played Laertes to Kenneth Branagh's Hamlet (1992–1993). In Iris (2001), he played the young John Bayley opposite Kate Winslet, with his performance lauded by critics and receiving a BAFTA nomination for Best Supporting Actor. Bonneville played Mr. Brown in the 2014 film Paddington and its 2017 sequel Paddington 2. He has appeared in the singing comedic role of The Pirate King in the ABC fairy tale-themed musical comedy extravaganza series Galavant during its 2015 and 2016 seasons. He also narrated the ITV series The Cruise. Bonneville has also narrated several Paddington stories available as audio books.

BRITISH DEATHS

Roland Pertwee born 15th May 1885 – 26th April 1963 was an English playwright, film and television screenwriter, director and actor. He was the father of Doctor Who actor Jon Pertwee and fellow playwright and screenwriter Michael Pertwee. He was also the second cousin of actor Bill Pertwee and grandfather of actors Sean Pertwee and Dariel Pertwee. From the 1910s to 1950s, he worked as a writer on many British films, providing either the basic story or full screenplay. He was one of numerous writers working on the script of A Yank at Oxford starring Robert Taylor and Vivien Leigh, the film in which his son Jon made his screen debut, and on Caravan. In 1954, he and his elder son Michael created The Grove Family – generally regarded as being the first soap opera on British television – for the BBC. A film version, entitled It's a Great Day, was produced in 1955, likewise written by the Pertwee's.

Admiral of the Fleet Andrew Browne Cunningham, 1st Viscount Cunningham of Hyndhope, KT, GCB, OM, DSO & Two Bars born 7th January 1883 – 12 June 1963 was a senior officer of the Royal Navy during the Second World War. He was widely known by his initials, "ABC". Andrew Cunningham was born in Rathmines in the south side of Dublin on 7 January 1883. After starting his schooling in Dublin and Edinburgh, he enrolled at Stubbington House School, at the age of ten. He entered the Royal Navy in 1897 as a naval cadet in the officers' training ship Britannia, passing out in 1898. He commanded a destroyer during the First World War and through most of the interwar period. He was awarded the Distinguished Service Order and two Bars, for his performance during this time, specifically for his actions in the Dardanelles and in the Baltics. In the Second World War, as Commander-in-Chief, Mediterranean Fleet, Cunningham led British naval forces to victory in several critical Mediterranean naval battles.

Sir John Berry Hobbs was born 16th December 1882 – 21st December 1963 and always known as Jack Hobbs, was an English professional cricketer who played for Surrey from 1905 to 1934 and for England in 61 Test matches between 1908 and 1930. Known as "The Master", he is regarded by critics as one of the greatest batsmen in the history of cricket. He is the leading run-scorer and century-maker in first-class cricket, with 61,237 runs and 197 centuries. A right-handed batsman and an occasional right-arm medium pace bowler, Hobbs also excelled as a fielder, particularly in the position of cover point. Hobbs' success was based on fast footwork, an ability to play many different shots, and excellent placement of the ball. Among the first batsmen to succeed against previously devastating googly bowlers, he adapted his technique to meet the new styles of bowling that arose early in his career; he mixed classical shots with an effective defence. He was Knighted in 1953, the first professional cricketer to be so honoured.

SPORTING EVENTS 1963

1963 County Cricket Season

The 1963 County Championship was the 64th officially organised running of the County Championship. Yorkshire won their second consecutive Championship title.
The method for deciding the championship was changed as follows -

Most points to determine champions
Follow on restored
One-day rules apply if the first two-thirds of playing time lost due to weather
10 points for a win
5 points for a tie
2 points for first innings lead in a drawn or lost match
1 point for a tie on first innings in a match drawn or lost
6 points for a win under one day rules

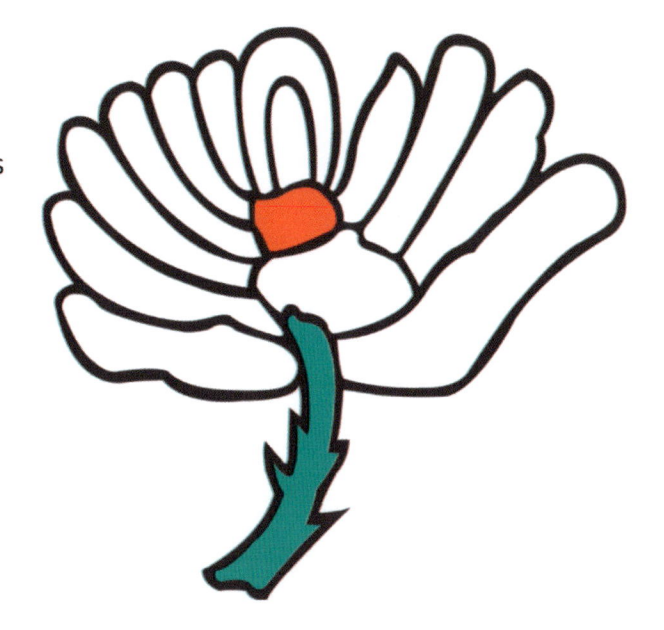

Position	Team	Played	Won	Lost	Drawn	No Dec	1st inn lead match L	1st inn lead match D	Points
1	Yorkshire	28	13	3	11	1	1	6	144
2	Glamorgan	28	11	8	8	1	1	6	124
3	Somerset	28	10	6	11	1	2	7	118
=4	Sussex	28	10	6	12	0	1	7	116
=4	Warwickshire	28	10	3	14	1	1	7	116
6	Middlesex	28	9	5	11	3	1	7	106
7	Northamptonshire	28	9	8	11	0	1	5	105
8	Gloucestershire	28	9	7	11	1	2	3	100
9	Nottinghamshire	28	6	8	13	1	4	7	82
10	Hampshire	28	7	8	10	3	1	4	80
11	Surrey	28	5	6	17	0	1	11	74
12	Essex	28	6	4	17	1	0	5	70
13	Kent	28	5	6	17	0	1	8	68
14	Worcestershire	28	4	8	13	3	2	8	60
15	Lancashire	28	4	10	13	1	2	7	58
16	Leicestershire	28	3	13	10	2	2	3	40
17	Derbyshire	28	2	14	9	3	1	3	28

1962–63 in English football

In a First Division season with heavy fixture congestion brought about by a severe winter, Everton emerged as league champions – their first piece of post-war silverware.

Tottenham Hotspur continued their brilliant start to the 1960s, finishing runners-up in the First Division and going on to lift the European Cup Winners' Cup to become English football's first winners of a European trophy. Burnley, the 1960 league champions, finished third. Leicester City, still yet to win a major trophy, emerge as surprise double challengers but eventually had to settle for a fourth-place finish in the league, and lost to Manchester United in the FA Cup final – with Matt Busby's rebuilding scheme paying off with the success being United's first trophy since the Munich air disaster five years earlier.

Pos	Team	Pld	W	D	L	GF	GA	GR	Pts
1	Everton	42	25	11	6	84	42	2.000	61
2	Tottenham Hotspur	42	23	9	10	111	62	1.790	55
3	Burnley	42	22	10	10	78	57	1.368	54
4	Leicester City	42	20	12	10	79	53	1.491	52
5	Wolverhampton Wanderers	42	20	10	12	93	65	1.431	50
6	Sheffield Wednesday	42	19	10	13	77	63	1.222	48
7	Arsenal	42	18	10	14	86	77	1.117	46
8	Liverpool	42	17	10	15	71	59	1.203	44
9	Nottingham Forest	42	17	10	15	67	69	0.971	44
10	Sheffield United	42	16	12	14	58	60	0.967	44
11	Blackburn Rovers	42	15	12	15	79	71	1.113	42
12	West Ham United	42	14	12	16	73	69	1.058	40
13	Blackpool	42	13	14	15	58	64	0.906	40
14	West Bromwich Albion	42	16	7	19	71	79	0.899	39
15	Aston Villa	42	15	8	19	62	68	0.912	38
16	Fulham	42	14	10	18	50	71	0.704	38
17	Ipswich Town	42	12	11	19	59	78	0.756	35
18	Bolton Wanderers	42	15	5	22	55	75	0.733	35
19	Manchester United	42	12	10	20	67	81	0.827	34
20	Birmingham City	42	10	13	19	63	90	0.700	33
21	Manchester City	42	10	11	21	58	102	0.569	31
22	Leyton Orient	42	6	9	27	37	81	0.457	21

1962–63 Scottish Division One

The 1962–63 Scottish Division One was won by Rangers by nine points over nearest rival Kilmarnock. Clyde and Raith Rovers finished 17th and 18th respectively and were relegated to the 1963-64 Second Division.

Rangers is the second-most successful club in world football in terms of trophies won, behind only Egyptian club Al Ahly. The club has won the Scottish League title 55 times, a domestic league joint world record, the Scottish Cup 33 times, the Scottish League Cup a record 27 times and the domestic treble on seven occasions, a joint world record shared with rivals Celtic. Rangers won the European Cup Winners' Cup in 1972 after being losing finalists twice, in 1961 (the first British club to reach a UEFA tournament final) and 1967. A third runners-up finish in European competition came in the UEFA Cup in 2008.

Pos	Team	Pld	W	D	L	GF	GA	GR	Pts
1	Rangers (C)	34	25	7	2	94	28	3.357	57
2	Kilmarnock	34	20	8	6	92	40	2.300	48
3	Partick Thistle	34	20	6	8	66	44	1.500	46
4	Celtic	34	19	6	9	76	44	1.727	44
5	Hearts	34	17	9	8	85	59	1.441	43
6	Aberdeen	34	17	7	10	70	47	1.489	41
7	Dundee United	34	15	11	8	67	52	1.288	41
8	Dunfermline	34	13	8	13	50	47	1.064	34
9	Dundee	34	12	9	13	60	49	1.224	33
10	Motherwell	34	10	11	13	60	63	0.952	31
11	Airdrieonians	34	14	2	18	52	76	0.684	30
12	St Mirren	34	10	8	16	52	72	0.722	28
13	Falkirk	34	12	3	19	54	69	0.783	27
14	Third Lanark	34	9	8	17	56	68	0.824	26
15	Queen of the South	34	10	6	18	36	75	0.480	26
16	Hibernian	34	8	9	17	47	67	0.701	25
17	Clyde (R)	34	9	5	20	49	83	0.590	23
18	Raith Rovers (R)	34	2	5	27	35	118	0.297	9

1963 Five Nations Championship

The 1963 Five Nations Championship was the thirty-fourth series of the rugby union Five Nations Championship. Including the previous incarnations as the Home Nations and Five Nations, this was the sixty-ninth series of the northern hemisphere rugby union championship. Ten matches were played between 12 January and 23 March. It was contested by England, France, Ireland, Scotland and Wales. England won their 17th title.

Ireland v England finished 0-0, the first scoreless draw between both teams since 1910.

Table

Position	Nation	Played	Won	Drawn	Lost	For	Against	Difference	Table points
1	England	4	3	1	0	29	19	+10	7
2	France	4	2	0	2	40	25	+15	4
2	Scotland	4	2	0	2	22	22	0	4
4	Ireland	4	1	1	2	19	33	−14	3
5	Wales	4	1	0	3	21	32	−11	2

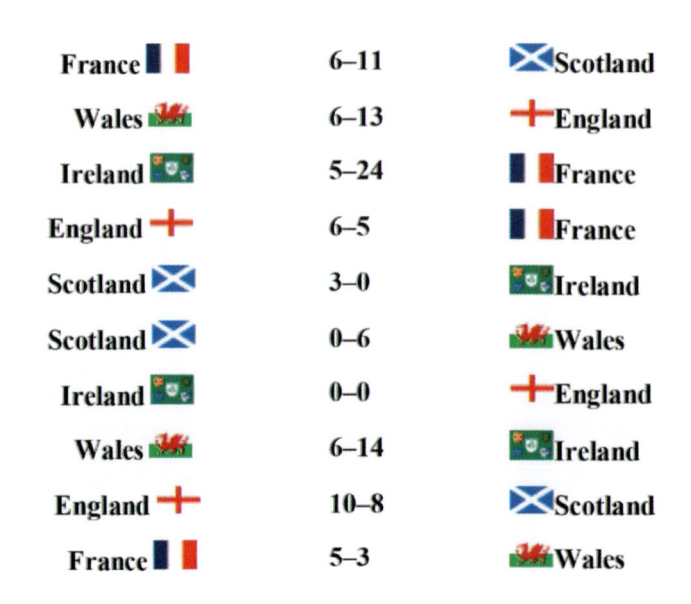

France	6–11	Scotland
Wales	6–13	England
Ireland	5–24	France
England	6–5	France
Scotland	3–0	Ireland
Scotland	0–6	Wales
Ireland	0–0	England
Wales	6–14	Ireland
England	10–8	Scotland
France	5–3	Wales

The Open 1963

The 1963 Open Championship was the 92nd Open Championship, held from 10th – 13th July at Royal Lytham & St Anne's Golf Club in Lytham St Anne's, England.

Bob Charles won his only major championship in a 36-hole playoff on Saturday, eight strokes ahead of runner-up Phil Rodgers, and became the first left-hander to win a major title. Masters winner Jack Nicklaus bogeyed the last two holes and came in third, one stroke out of the playoff. A heavy favourite among the local bettors, two-time defending champion Arnold Palmer tied for 26th. U.S. Open champion Julius Boros did not play.

This was the last 36-hole playoff at The Open, the format was changed to 18 holes the following year, used in 1970 and 1975. The four-hole aggregate format was introduced in 1986 and first used in 1989.

Place	Player	Country	Score	To par	Money (£)
T1	Bob Charles	New Zealand	68-72-66-71=277	-3	Playoff
T1	Phil Rodgers	United States	67-68-73-69=277	-3	Playoff
3	Jack Nicklaus	United States	71-67-70-70=278	-2	800
4	Kel Nagle	Australia	69-70-73-71=283	+3	650
5	Peter Thomson	Australia	67-69-71-78=285	+5	500
6	Christy O'Connor Snr	Ireland	74-68-76-68=286	+6	350
T7	Gary Player	South Africa	75-70-72-70=287	+7	250
T7	Ramón Sota	Spain	69-73-73-72=287	+7	250
T9	Jean Garaïalde	France	72-69-72-75=288	+8	163
T9	Sebastián Miguel	Spain	73-69-73-73=288	+8	163

Playoff
Saturday, 13th July 1963

Charles won the 36-hole playoff by eight strokes; he led by three after the first round.

Place	Player	Country	Score	To par	Money (£)
1	**Bob Charles**	New Zealand	69-71=140	E	1,500
2	Phil Rodgers	United States	72-76=148	+8	1,000

Grand National 1963

The 1963 Grand National was the 117th renewal of the Grand National horse race that took place at Aintree Racecourse near Liverpool, England, on 30 March 1963.

The race was won narrowly by 66/1 shot Ayala, ridden by 19-year-old jockey Pat Buckley. Forty-seven horses ran and all returned safely to the stables. Ayala was jointly owned by his trainer, Keith Piggott, father of Lester Piggott, and by Raymond Bessone, the hairdresser also known as Teasy-Weasy. Piggott's father (and Lester's grandfather), Ernie, rode the winners of the National in 1912 and 1919.

Triple Crown Winners 1963

2,000 Guineas

Only for Life (1960–1985) was a British Thoroughbred racehorse and sire. In a career that lasted from September 1962 to summer 1964 he ran ten times and won three races. A horse who was particularly effective on soft ground, Only for Life recorded his most significant victory when he won the 2000 Guineas at Newmarket in 1963 as a 33/1 outsider. His other major win came in June that year in the King Edward VII Stakes at Royal Ascot. He was retired to stud in 1964 and was later exported to Japan where he died in 1985.

St Leger

Ragusa. On his first appearance of the 1963 season, Ragusa was sent to England, where he started favourite for the Dee Stakes at Chester Racecourse but finished second to My Myosotis. In June, he started a 25/1 outsider for the Derby at Epsom and exceeded expectations by finishing third of the twenty-six runners behind Relko and Merchant Venturer. At the Curragh later that month, Ragusa won the Irish Derby by two and a half lengths after Relko was withdrawn at the start. In July, Ragusa started at odds of 4/1 in a field of ten runners for Britain's most prestigious all-aged race, he King George VI and Queen Elizabeth Stakes at Ascot. He won by four lengths from the four-year-old Miralgo. At York Racecourse in August, he defeated the 2000 Guineas winner Only for Life in the Great Voltigeur Stakes at odds of 2/5. At Doncaster Racecourse in September, Ragusa started the 2/5 favourite for the St Leger and won in a canter by six lengths.

The Derby

Relko. At Epsom on 29th May, Relko was sent off the 5/1 favourite in a field of twenty-six runners. Ridden by the 21-year-old Yves Saint-Martin, Relko tracked the leading group in the early stages before moving up into third place early in the straight. He was moved up to take the lead from Tarqogan three furlongs from the finish and pulled away from the rest of the field to win easily by six lengths from Merchant Venturer and Ragusa. The slow winning time of 2:39.4 was explained by the rain-softened state of the turf. Relko's Derby win was overshadowed for some time because of the revelation by the Daily Express that he had failed a drugs test. The incident took place in the context of a series of investigations into the "doping" of horses in British races. It was not until October that the Jockey Club confirmed Relko as the winner, stating that the substances detected could not be positively identified and therefore could not be proved to have affected the result. At the end of June, Relko was scheduled to run in the Irish Derby and made 11/8 favourite, but was withdrawn from the race minutes before the start, after appearing to be lame, leading to further suspicions of foul play.

1963 British Grand Prix

The 1963 British Grand Prix was a Formula One motor race held at the Silverstone Circuit in Northamptonshire, England on 20th July 1963. It was race 5 of 10 in both the 1963 World Championship of Drivers and the 1963 International Cup for Formula One Manufacturers.

It was also the eighteenth British Grand Prix, and the first to be held at Silverstone since 1960. The race was won by Jim Clark for the second year in succession driving a Lotus 25.

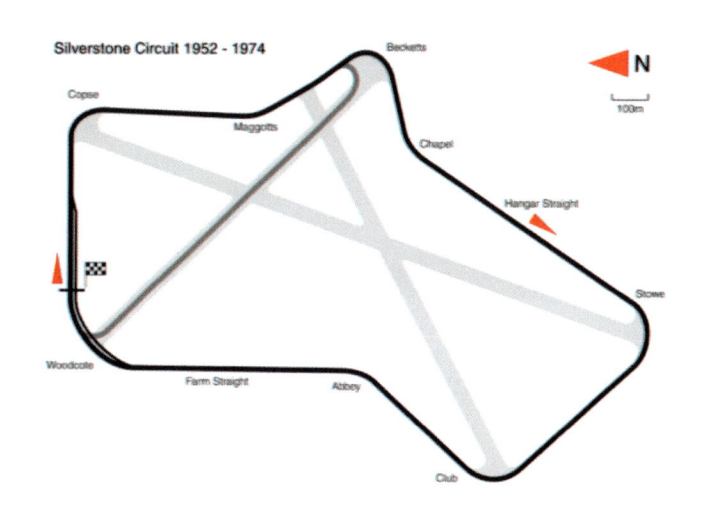

Final Placings

Pos	No	Driver	Constructor	Laps	Time/Retired	Grid	Points
1	4	Jim Clark	Lotus-Climax	82	2:14:09.6	1	9
2	10	John Surtees	Ferrari	82	+ 25.8	5	6
3	1	Graham Hill	BRM	82	+ 37.6	3	4
4	2	Richie Ginther	BRM	81	+ 1 lap	9	3
5	3	Lorenzo Bandini	BRM	81	+ 1 lap	8	2
6	12	Jim Hall	Lotus-BRM	80	+ 2 laps	13	1
7	19	Chris Amon	Lola-Climax	80	+ 2 laps	14	
8	20	Mike Hailwood	Lotus-Climax	78	+ 4 laps	17	
9	7	Tony Maggs	Cooper-Climax	78	+ 4 laps	7	
10	23	Carel Godin de Beaufort	Porsche	76	+ 6 laps	21	
11	21	Masten Gregory	Lotus-BRM	75	+ 7 laps	22	
12	22	Bob Anderson	Lola-Climax	75	+ 7 laps	16	
13	24	John Campbell-Jones	Lola-Climax	74	+ 8 laps	23	

Race details

Date	20 July 1963
Official	XVI RAC British Grand Prix
Location	Silverstone Circuit
Course	Permanent racing facility
Course	4.711 km (2.927 mi)
Distance	82 laps, 386.261 km (240.011 mi)
Weather	Warm, dry and sunny

Pole position

Driver	Jim Clark	Lotus-Climax
Time	1:34.4	

Fastest lap

Driver	John Surtees	Ferrari
Time	1:36.0 on lap 3	

Podium

First	Jim Clark	Lotus-Climax
Second	John Surtees	Ferrari
Third	Graham Hill	BRM

1963 Wimbledon Championships

The 1963 Wimbledon Championships took place on the outdoor grass courts at the All England Lawn Tennis and Croquet Club in Wimbledon, London, United Kingdom. It was the 77th staging of the Wimbledon Championships, and the third Grand Slam tennis event of 1963. The tournament which was scheduled from 24 June until 6 July was played in cold and wet weather conditions. Play on the final Saturday was cancelled due to rain and the women's singles, the men's and women's doubles and the mixed doubles finals were concluded on Monday, 8th July. This edition of the tournament saw the introduction of the regulation that player's clothing must be predominantly white.

Men's Singles

Chuck McKinley defeated Fred Stolle 9–7, 6–1, 6–4 in the final to win the gentlemen's singles tennis title at the 1963 Wimbledon Championships. Rod Laver was the defending champion, but was ineligible to compete after turning professional.

Women's Singles

First-seeded Margaret Smith defeated unseeded Billie Jean Moffitt in the final, 6–3, 6–4 to win the ladies' singles tennis title at the 1963 Wimbledon Championships and completed the career grand slam in singles. Karen Susman did not defend her title as she was expecting her first child.

Men's Doubles

Bob Hewitt and Fred Stolle were the defending champions, but lost in the third round to Michael Hann and Roger Taylor. Rafael Osuna and Antonio Palafox defeated Jean-Claude Barclay and Pierre Darmon in the final, 4–6, 6–2, 6–2, 6–2 to win the Gentlemen' Doubles tennis title at the 1963 Wimbledon Championship.

Women's Doubles

Billie Jean Moffitt and Karen Susman were the defending champions, but Susman did not compete as she was expecting her first child. Moffitt partnered with Carole Caldwell but lost in the second round to Deidre Catt and Liz Starkie. Maria Bueno and Darlene Hard defeated Robyn Ebbern and Margaret Smith in the final, 8–6, 9–7 to win the Ladies' Doubles tennis title at the 1963 Wimbledon Championships.

Mixed Doubles

Neale Fraser and Margaret duPont were the defending champions, but did not compete. Ken Fletcher and Margaret Smith defeated Bob Hewitt and Darlene Hard in the final, 11–9, 6–4 to win the Mixed Doubles tennis title at the 1963 Wimbledon Championships.

Chuck Mckinley

Margaret Smith

BOOKS PUBLISHED IN 1963

The Clocks is a work of detective fiction by British writer Agatha Christie, first published in the UK by the Collins Crime Club on 7th November 1963 and in the US by Dodd, Mead and Company the following year. It features the Belgian detective Hercule Poirot. The UK edition retailed at sixteen shillings (16/-) and the US edition at $4.50.

In the novel Poirot never visits any of the crime scenes or speaks to any of the witnesses or suspects. He is challenged to prove his claim that a crime can be solved by the exercise of the intellect alone.

The novel marks the return of partial first-person narrative, a technique that Christie had largely abandoned earlier in the Poirot sequence but which she had employed in the previous Ariadne Oliver novel, The Pale Horse (1961). There are two interwoven plots: the mystery Poirot works on from his armchair while the police work on the spot, and a Cold War spy story told in the first-person narrative.

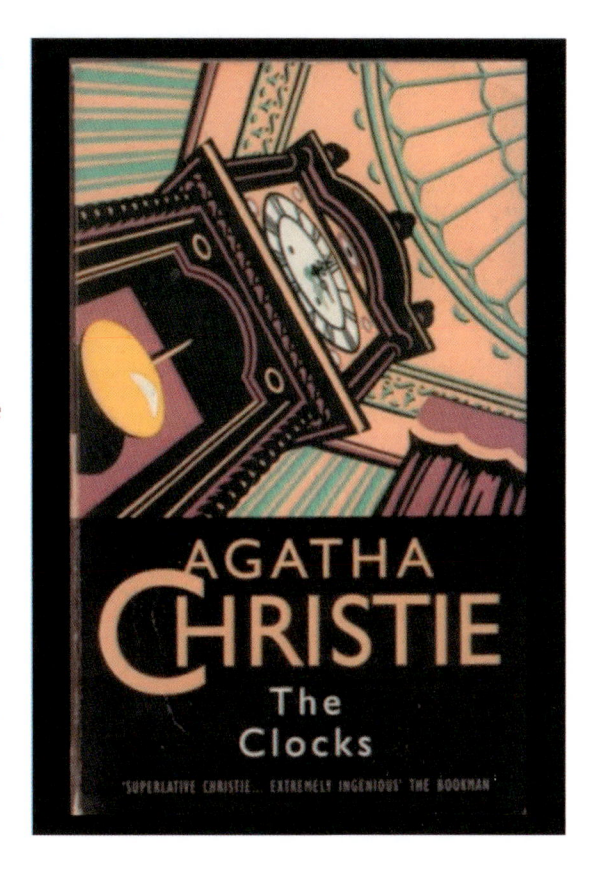

On Her Majesty's Secret Service is the tenth novel in Ian Fleming's James Bond series, first published in the UK by Jonathan Cape on 1st April 1963. The initial and secondary print runs sold out, with over 60,000 books sold in the first month. Fleming wrote the book in Jamaica whilst the first film in the Eon Productions series of films, Dr. No, was being filmed nearby. On Her Majesty's Secret Service is the second book in what is known as the "Blofeld trilogy", which begins with Thunderball and concludes with You Only Live Twice. The story centres on Bond's ongoing search to find Ernst Stavro Blofeld after the Thunderball incident; through contact with the College of Arms in London Bond finds Blofeld based in Switzerland. After meeting him and discovering his latest plans, Bond attacks the centre where he is based, although Blofeld escapes in the confusion. Bond meets and falls in love with Contessa Teresa "Tracy" di Vicenzo during the story. The pair marry at the end of the story but Blofeld kills Bond's wife, hours after the ceremony.

On Her Majesty's Secret Service received broadly good reviews in the British and American press.

The Collector is a 1963 thriller novel by English author John Fowles, in his literary debut. Its plot follows a lonely, psychotic young man who kidnaps a female art student in London and holds her captive in the cellar of his rural farmhouse. Divided in two sections, the novel contains both the perspective of the captor, Frederick, and that of Miranda, the captive. The novel is about a lonely young man, Frederick Clegg, who works as a clerk in a city hall and collects butterflies in his spare time. The first part of the novel tells the story from his point of view.

Alan Pryce-Jones of The New York Times wrote of the novel: "John Fowles is a very brave man. He has written a novel which depends for its effect on total acceptance by the reader. There is no room in it for the least hesitation, the smallest false note, for not only is it written in the first person singular, but its protagonist is a very special case indeed. Mr. Fowles's main skill is in his use of language. There is not a false note in his delineation of Fred." Hayden Carruth of the Press & Sun-Bulletin praised the novel as "brisk" and "professional," adding that Fowles "knows how to evoke the oblique horror of innocence as well as the direct horror of knowledge."

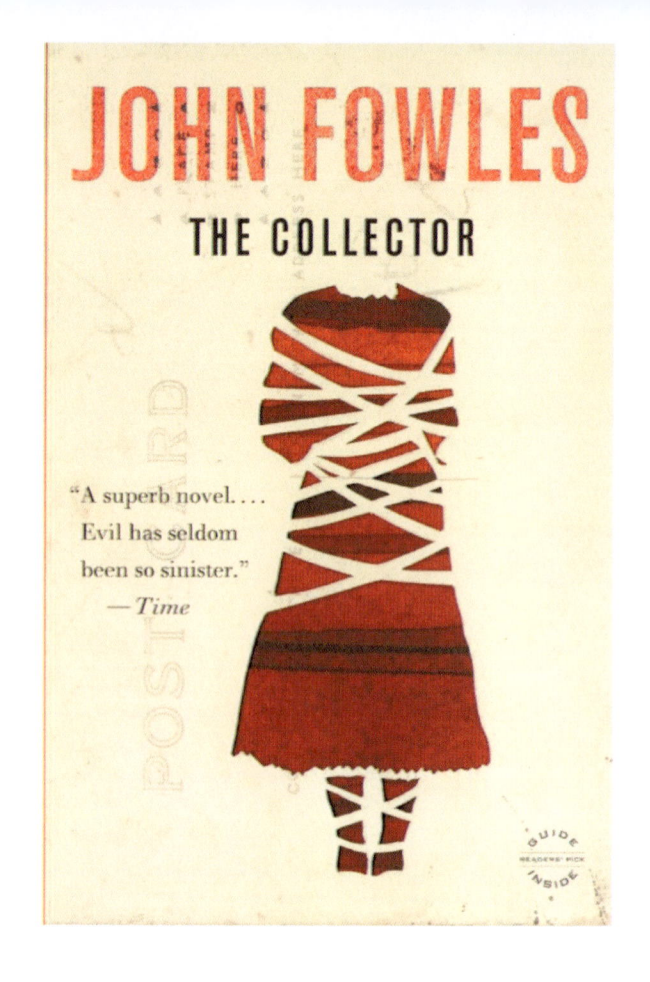

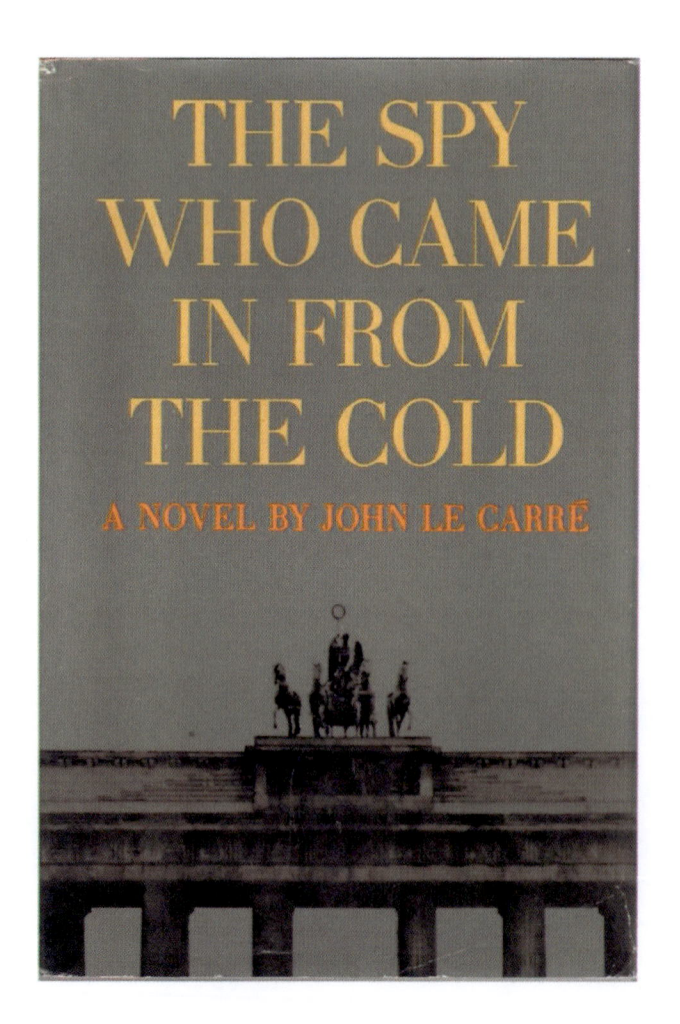

The Spy Who Came in from the Cold is a 1963 Cold War spy novel by the British author John le Carré. It depicts Alec Leamas, a British agent, being sent to East Germany as a faux defector to sow disinformation about a powerful East German intelligence officer. It serves as a sequel to le Carré's previous novels Call for the Dead and A Murder of Quality, which also featured the fictitious British intelligence organization, "The Circus", and its agents George Smiley and Peter Guillam. The Spy Who Came in from the Cold occurs during the heightened tensions that characterised the late 1950s and early 1960s Cold War, when a Warsaw Pact–NATO war sparked in Germany seemed likely. The story begins and concludes in Berlin, about a year after the completion of the Berlin Wall and around the time when double-agent Heinz Felfe was exposed and tried. The Spy Who Came in from the Cold picks up two years later, where Mundt has had a somewhat meteoric rise to become the head of the Abteilung, because of his success with counter-intelligence operations against British networks, as well as a member of the Presidium of the Socialist Unity Party. Characters and events from The Spy Who Came in from the Cold are reinvestigated in A Legacy of Spies, le Carré's 2017 novel centring on an aging Guillam.

Ice Station Zebra is a 1963 thriller novel written by Scottish author Alistair MacLean. It marked a return to MacLean's classic Arctic setting. After completing this novel, whose plot line parallels real-life events during the Cold War, MacLean retired from writing for three years. Drift ice Station Zebra, a British meteorological station built on an ice floe in the Arctic Sea, suffers a catastrophic oil fire; several of its men die, and their shelter and supplies are destroyed. The survivors hole up in one hut with little food and heat. The novel was influenced by the heightened atmosphere of the Cold War, with its escalating series of international crises in the late 1950s and early 1960s, such as the U-2 incident; West Berlin; unrest in Hungary, Indochina, Congo, and Latin America; and the Cuban Missile Crisis.

The novel exploits contemporary fascination with the under-the-ice exploits of such American nuclear-powered submarines as Nautilus (first to pass under the North Pole), Skate, Sargo and Seadragon. MacLean may have been anticipating the excitement of his British readers regarding the upcoming commissioning of HMS Dreadnought, the Royal Navy's first nuclear submarine.

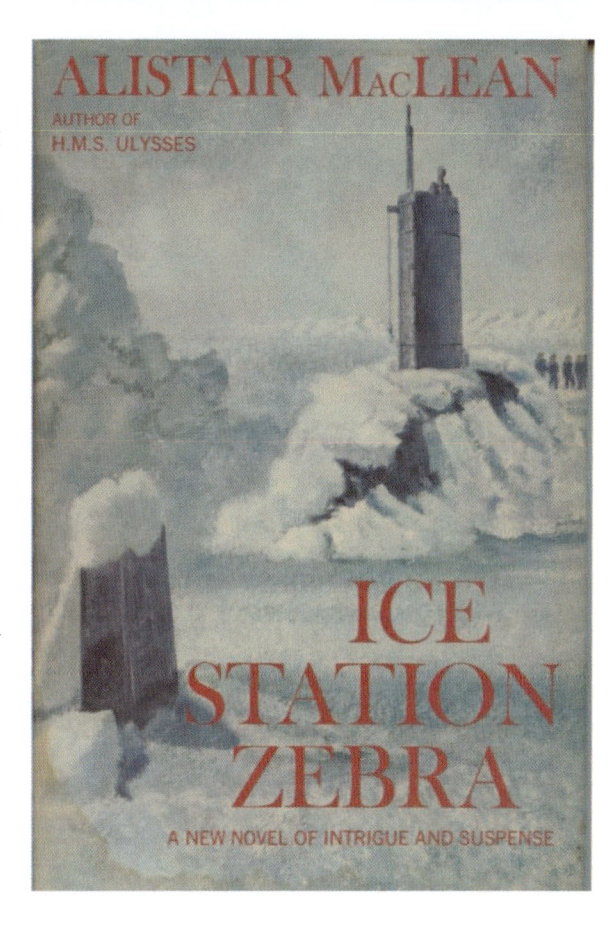

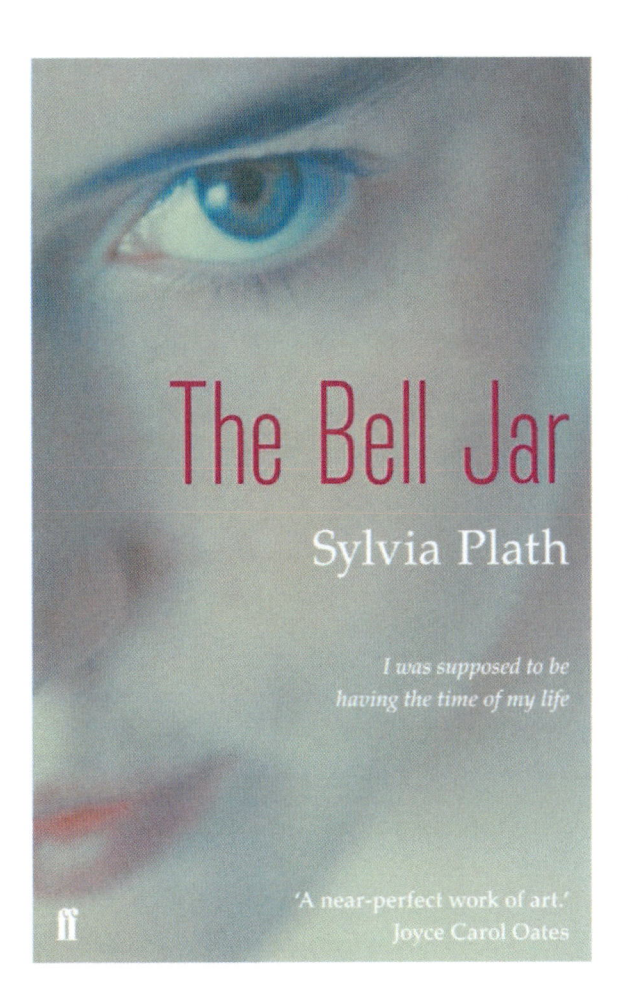

The Bell Jar is the only novel written by the American writer and poet Sylvia Plath. Originally published under the pseudonym "Victoria Lucas" in 1963, the novel is semi-autobiographical with the names of places and people changed. The book is often regarded as a roman à clef because the protagonist's descent into mental illness parallels Plath's own experiences with what may have been clinical depression or bipolar II disorder. Plath died by suicide a month after its first United Kingdom publication. The novel was published under Plath's name for the first time in 1967 and was not published in the United States until 1971, in accordance with the wishes of both Plath's husband, Ted Hughes, and her mother. The novel has been translated into nearly a dozen languages.

According to her husband, Plath began writing the novel in 1961, after publishing The Colossus, her first collection of poetry. Plath finished writing the novel in August 1961. After she separated from Hughes, Plath moved to a smaller flat in London, "giving her time and place to work uninterruptedly. Then at top speed and with very little revision from start to finish she wrote The Bell Jar," he explained.

MOVIE'S 1963

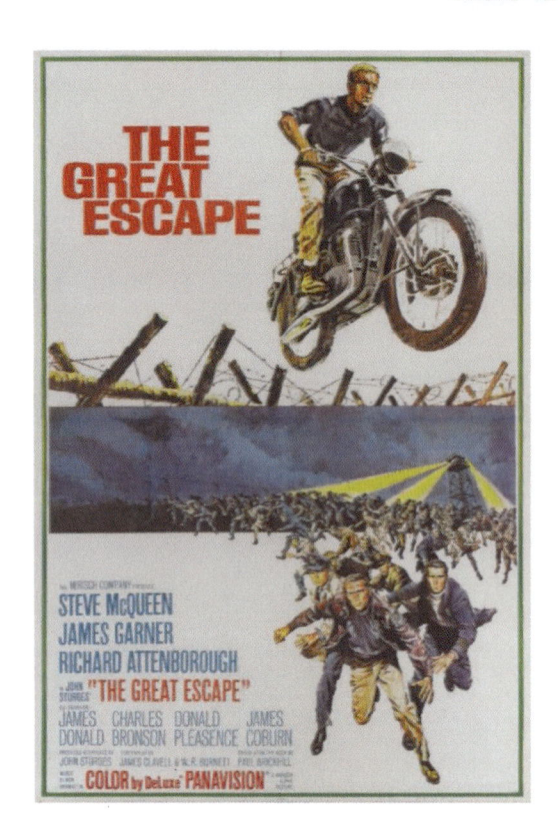

The Great Escape. In 1942, the Germans have built what they consider an escape-proof P.O.W. camp, where they plan to house all the problem P.O.W.s (those that have made multiple escape attempts in the past). What the Germans don't realize is that they've put all the best escape minds in one location. If they can't escape, these P.O.W.s believe it is their military duty to make the enemy place as much effort into their confinement as possible to divert them from other war-related pursuits. Royal Air Force Squadron Leader Bartlett plans not just a one or two man escape at a time like most escape attempts in the past have been, but a massive escape of two hundred fifty men through a series of tunnels. If one tunnel is found, they can focus on the others. Each escapee will be provided with a complete set of forged documents and standard clothing. With their reputations preceding them, each P.O.W. is assigned a specific task in carrying out the plan. Somewhat outside of the plot are Captain Hilts and Flying Officer Ives, who spent their first thirty days in camp in the cooler together.

Run time is 2h 52mins

Trivia

In this movie, several Americans (including Hilts and Henley) were amongst the escapees. In real-life, American officers assisted with the construction of the escape tunnel, but weren't amongst the escapees, because the Germans moved them to a remote compound just before the escape.

Several cast members were actual POWs during World War II. Donald Pleasence was held in the German camp Stalag Luft I, Hannes Messemer in a Russian camp, and Til Kiwe and Hans Reiser were prisoners of the Americans. Pleasence said the set was a very accurate representation of a POW camp.

Charles Bronson, who portrays the chief tunneler, brought his own expertise and experiences to the set. He had been a coal miner before turning to acting, and gave director John Sturges advice on how to move the dirt. As a result of his work in the coal mines, Bronson suffered from claustrophobia, just as his character had.

Goofs

The motorcycle that Hilts uses in his escape attempt was a 1960s British Triumph 650.

The transport truck carrying the 50 prisoners who are to be shot has modern brake lights, circa early 1960's. Military trucks, especially during the war, either had no brake lights or taillights or only one very small red light at the rear.

In an early scene after the prisoners are brought into the camp, Werner asks Hendley why an American would fight alongside Britain, since they burned down the U.S. capital in 1812. While it happened during the War of 1812, the burning of Washington occurred in 1814.

Charade. A stunning Audrey Hepburn's Regina Lambert - the wife of a man named Charles. Upon her return to Paris from a ski holiday in a stunning Audrey Hepburn is Regina Lambert - the wife of a man named Charles. Upon her return to Paris from a ski holiday, in Megève, she finds her husband's been murdered, and their apartment stripped bare. She's told by CIA agent Hamilton Bartholemew that Charles Lambert was one of a group of men who stole a quarter of a million dollars in gold from the U.S. government during World War II, and the government wants it back. The money was not found amongst his few possessions, and Regina can't shed any light on its whereabouts. She's soon visited by Peter Joshua (a debonair Cary Grant) whom she'd briefly met whilst in Megève. When her husband's former partners (in crime), who were double-crossed by Charles, begin to terrorize her for the money, Peter offers to help Regina find it. So, begins an elaborate charade, in which nothing - and no one - is who, or what they seem to be.

Run time 1h 53mins

Trivia

It was agreed Cary Grant would keep all of his clothes on when he took a shower, as he was nearly sixty and slightly overweight. However, they then decided the scene was funnier that way.

Due to the suspense, the presence of Cary Grant, the structure of the screenplay, and the frequent plot twists, many people believe this was a Sir Alfred Hitchcock film. Hitchcock was not involved in the making of the film at all. This confusion has prompted fans of the film to call it "the best Hitchcock film Hitchcock never made."

Seven studios rejected the original screenplay. Screenwriter Peter Stone turned it into a novel which was serialized in Redbook, which in turn sparked interest from all seven studios.

Goofs

Scobie is covering "Dyle" with a gun held in his artificial hand/claw, but it wouldn't be threatening as there's no way he would be able to pull the trigger.

When Regina is taken to the morgue to identify her husband's body, the coroner's hands are visible as the body drawer is closed. The coroner's fingers would have prevented the drawer from closing or else his fingers would have been injured.

When Audrey Hepburn and Cary Grant arrive at the stamp market, workers on ladders can be seen starting to put a new cover on the completely roofless Berkeley Café in the background. However, a few minutes later, when Grant runs to catch a cab, the building is directly behind him, and the new roof is long since complete.

The lights on the Seine tour boat go out, but in the long shot they are still working.

The Birds. Melanie Daniels is the modern rich socialite, part of the jet-set who always gets what she wants. When lawyer Mitch Brenner sees her in a pet shop, he plays something of a practical joke on her, and she decides to return the favour. She drives about an hour north of San Francisco to Bodega Bay, where Mitch spends the weekends with his mother Lydia and younger sister Cathy. Soon after her arrival, however, the birds in the area begin to act strangely.

A seagull attacks Melanie as she is crossing the bay in a small boat, and then, Lydia finds her neighbour dead, obviously the victim of a bird attack. Soon, birds in the hundreds and thousands are attacking anyone they find out of doors.

There is no explanation as to why this might be happening, and as the birds continue their vicious attacks, survival becomes the priority.

Run time 1h 59mins

Trivia

When audiences left the U.K. premiere at the Odeon, Leicester Square, London, they were greeted by the sound of screeching and flapping birds from loudspeakers hidden in the trees to scare them further.

Alfred Hitchcock revealed on The Dick Cavett Show (1968) that 3,200 birds were trained for the movie. He said the ravens were the cleverest, and the seagulls were the most vicious.

Several endings were being considered. One that was considered would have shown the Golden Gate Bridge completely covered by birds.

The schoolhouse in this movie is the Potter Schoolhouse, which served Bodega, California from 1873 to 1961. The building is now a private residence.

Goofs

Invited to the Brenner's' for dinner, Melanie plays the piano while Cathy talks to her. But Melanie's fingers don't match the melody, especially the right hand's higher notes.

During the bird attack on the house, Melanie falls back, almost swooning and crushes a lamp-shade. But, during the rest of the movie, the lampshade remains in perfect condition.

When the gas station attendant is hit by a gull, he falls face down, and his body is angled toward the camera. Mitch and some other men go to help him, and in the last shot of them together, he is face up and his body is angled to the left. There is quick cutting in this sequence, and not enough time between shots for the men to have moved the attendant.

Twice in the movie, a kettle and serving carafe clearly show multiple bright studio lights reflected in them.

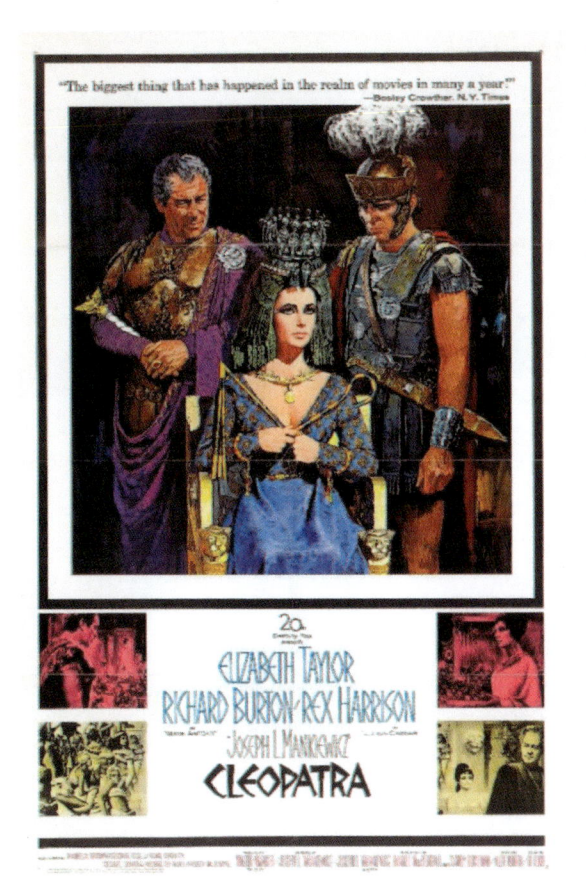

Cleopatra. Epic saga of the legendary Queen's reign from the time Julius Caesar (Sir Rex Harrison) arrived in Egypt until her death around eighteen years later. Cleopatra (Dame Elizabeth Taylor) is portrayed as a schemer, firstly to gain control over the Egyptian kingdom from her brother with whom she ruled jointly. Having gained the confidence of Caesar, they become lovers and she bears him the son he never had. Her attempts at ensuring that the boy takes his rightful place in Rome are thwarted when Caesar is assassinated and she flees back to Egypt. Many years later, Marc Antony (Richard Burton), now responsible for the eastern half of the Roman Empire, seeks an alliance with Egypt. He and Cleopatra become lovers and form a military alliance, but are forced to retreat after losing a major naval encounter at Actium. Both eventually take their own lives.

Box Office
Budget: $44,000,000 (estimated)
Gross USA: $57,777,778

Run time 3h 12mins

Trivia
Writer and director Joseph L. Mankiewicz hoped that this movie would be released as two separate movies, "Caesar and Cleopatra", followed by "Antony and Cleopatra". Each was to run approximately three hours. Twentieth Century Fox decided against this and premiered the movie at 4 hours 3 minutes. More cuts pared the movie to three hours fourteen minutes for general release. It is hoped that the missing two hours will be located, and that one day a six-hour "Director's Cut" will be available.

Cleopatra's (Dame Elizabeth Taylor's) navy required huge numbers of boats and ships. It was said at the time that Twentieth Century Fox had the world's third largest navy.

When this movie finally broke even in 1973, Twentieth Century Fox "closed the books" on it, keeping all future profits secret to avoid paying those who might have been promised a percentage of the profits.

Goofs
At one-point Cleopatra talks to Caesar about Rome's interest in Egyptian corn. Ancient people in that part of the world did not know what corn / maize was, since it was originally cultivated in prehistoric Mesoamerica and spread worldwide only in the 15th and 16th centuries. However, British usage of the word "corn" refers to all cereal grain, including wheat, oats, and maize.

When Cleopatra is rolled out of the rug in her first appearance, she is wearing flat sandals. In the next shot, she walks to the table in high heels.

Cleopatra's arrival and procession would not have entered the Roman Forum itself, as portrayed in the movie, since during the Republic, all foreign rulers were prohibited from crossing the Pomerium, the sacred boundary of the city, into Rome proper.

It's a Mad Mad Mad Mad World. Somewhere in the desert. A car speeds like crazy along the roads. Suddenly, the driver loses control and sails off a cliff. Four other vehicles are near, they stop to help. The dying man narrates the drivers of a fortune in cash, $350,000, which he has hidden below a giant "W" in Santa Rosita, some 200 miles away.

The four drivers and their respective passengers can't decide on how to share the future fortune, and suddenly a wild race to Santa Rosita develops. While one party manages to rent a plane (from 1916), the others face different problems like tire damage, untrustworthy lifts, deep water, drunken millionaires, a British adventurer, little girl's bicycles, and last but far not least a mother-in-law from hell and her imbecile son. While the folks slowly travel towards the goal, they are being watched. Who ever said that nobody else knew about the fortune?

Box Office
Budget: $9,400,000 (estimated)

Run time 3h 30mins

Trivia

Jack Benny's cameo role was originally offered to Stan Laurel, but Laurel turned it down. When his best friend and partner Oliver Hardy died in 1957, he pledged never to perform again. He kept that promise for the rest of his life. By the time this happened, a long shot of the character had already been filmed with a stand-in wearing Laurel's trademark bowler hat. This is why Benny is seen wearing a bowler hat despite his never having worn one as part of his regular work.

When this film was made, there were about 100 stunt performers in the United States. About 80 of them worked on this film.

The film was so crammed with action that each leading actor was given two scripts: one for the dialogue and one for physical comedy.

Goofs

At the scene towards the end of the movie where Culpeper and the other two police cars meet at the beachfront, Culpeper tells the others he wants to handle it on his own. The other two police cars then reverse out and proceed straight through a red light.

In the far shot of Colonel Wilberforce falling off the air traffic control tower, we see the microphone he was holding dangling about a yard below him. But in the close-up, he is holding it again.

While in the airplane Crump smashes the windshield and other parts of the plane, but when they land, the plane is undamaged.

In the final scene at the gas station, Pike backs up the truck into the water tower that falls on the bathrooms that were destroyed in an earlier scene.

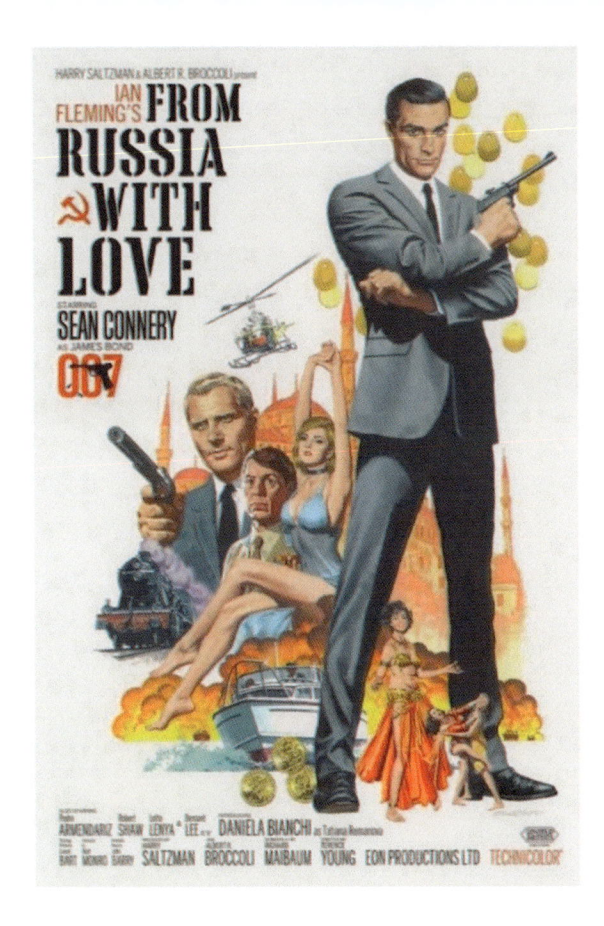

From Russia with Love. The S.P.E.C.T.R.E. Number 1 assigns the S.P.E.C.T.R.E. Number 3, Rosa Klebb, an ex S.M.E.R.S.H. operative before defecting from Russia, and the S.P.E.C.T.R.E. Number 5 and expert planner Kronsteen to plot a scheme to steal the Russian's Lektor decoder and revenge on James Bond for killing Dr. No. Rosa Klebb recruits the S.P.E.C.T.R.E. assassin Grant and lures the naive and loyal Russian Corporal State Security Tatiana Romanova, who works at the Soviet consulate in Istanbul and believes that Rosa Klebb still works for S.M.E.R.S.H.

Meanwhile, M summons James Bond and tells him that Tatiana wants to defect to London and has offered the Lektor as part of the bargain. However, she wants to go to England with Bond. Bond and M suspect that it might be a trap, but Bond sees Tatiana's photo and decides to go to Istanbul, where he has the support of the local operative Kerim Bey. He meets Tatiana and they plot a plan to steal the Lektor and return to London. But they do not know that they are actually pawns in the scheme plotted by S.P.E.C.T.R.E.

Run time 1h 55mins

Trivia

Then-President John F. Kennedy listed Ian Fleming's book as among his top ten favourite novels of all time. That list was published in Life Magazine on 17th March 1961. Possibly as a result, the producers decided to make this the second James Bond movie. According to the book "Death of a President" (1964) by William Raymond Manchester, this was the last movie J.F.K. ever saw, in a private screening in the White House, 20th November 1963.

This movie broke box-office records, and was responsible for launching Sir Sean Connery as a major star, rather than Dr. No (1962).

Final James Bond movie viewed by Ian Fleming.

Goofs

When Klebb arrives on SPECTRE island and asks where Grant is, the henchman says "At the lake" but his lips are saying something different. Klebb then says, "Take me to the lake" but her lips don't say lake either. In both cases it looks like they're saying the word "pool".

Making their escape by train, Bond and Tatiana are given cover documents to aid their escape. Bond tells Tatiana that they are Mr & Mrs David Somerset and that her cover name is Caroline. They briefly discuss the particulars of their cover identities and from that point on they should assume that they are being observed, so should always maintain their covers. Just a moment later, James opens the compartment door and loudly calls her "Tania". No well-trained spy would ever make such a basic mistake.

When "Q" is showing Bond the new tricked-out attaché case and its equipment, he explains the new "AR-7 folding sniper rifle". That rifle doesn't fold; it disassembles, and its components are stored within its stock.

The Pink Panther. The trademark of The Phantom, a renowned jewel thief, is a glove left at the scene of the crime. Inspector Clouseau, an expert on The Phantom's exploits, feels sure that he knows where The Phantom will strike next and leaves Paris for Switzerland, where the famous Lugashi jewel 'The Pink Panther' is going to be. However, he does not know who The Phantom really is, or for that matter who anyone else really is...

On the Phantom's trail is the klutzy French police inspector Jacques Clouseau (Peter Sellers) of the Sûreté, whose wife Simone (Capucine) is unknown to him the paramour of Charles and helper in the Phantom's crimes. Clouseau tries to stop the theft attempts, but he is so clueless and clumsy that when several attempts are made at a fancy-dress party, he looks everywhere but the right place. Throughout the film, scenes at the skiing resort's hotel show Madame Clouseau dodging her husband while trying both to carry out Sir Charles' plans and to avoid George, who is enamoured of her.

Run time 1h 55mins

Trivia

An animated Pink Panther was created for the opening credits because writer and director Blake Edwards felt that the credits would benefit from some kind of cartoon character. David H. DePatie and Friz Freleng decided to personify the film's eponymous jewel, and the Pink Panther character was chosen by Edwards from over a hundred alternative panther sketches. The Pink Panther introduced in the opening credits became a popular film and television character in his own right, beginning with the cartoon short The Pink Phink (1964) the following year.

When presenting at a subsequent Oscar Awards ceremony, David Niven requested his walk-on music be changed from the "Pink Panther" theme, as "that was not really my film."

In the bath scene with Capucine and Robert Wagner, an industrial-strength foaming agent is used, which burned both of the stars' skin. Wagner, who was completely immersed at one point, became blind for four weeks.

Goofs

When Sir Charles is first skiing behind Princess Dala to spy on her movements, he is wearing binoculars with the strap over his right shoulder, his left arm through the strap, and binoculars under his left arm as he skis with ski poles in both hands. When he stops, his left arm and ski pole are no longer through the strap; the binocular strap is simply around his neck with the binoculars hanging on his chest as he grabs them to look through them.

When Clouseau first opens the door to his room to look into the hall he yanks it open it swings halfway open then slams back into him. A small "stop" block can be seen fastened to the floor where the door can hit it. The block is gone in all other shots.

Jason and the Argonauts. An infant Jason is taken away far off safely after his family is killed and his father's throne taken by his uncle Pelias.

Jason returns aft 20 years to claim his rightful throne. He saves Pelias from drowning unknown to him that he is the killer of his family and usurper of his throne. But Pelias recognizes him and cunningly encourages Jason to sail off to the end of the world to seek the legendary golden fleece n later reclaim the kingdom and face Pelias.

Pelias gets relieved thinking that Jason won't be able to return safely. Jason is offered help by Zeus but he declines and sets out to build a ship and recruit the best men from all over Greece and among them is Hercules which boosts the morale of the crew.

Budget
$2,500,000 (estimated)

Run time 1h 44mins

Trivia

It took Ray Harryhausen four months to produce the skeleton scene, which runs, at most, three minutes.

John Cairney and Nigel Green didn't get along at all during filming. Green accused Cairney of being very effeminate. The last scene they filmed together was the scene in which Hercules and Hylas enter the treasure chamber, hidden in the plinth of the mighty Talos. The lighting used to give the treasure its sparkling effect was very bright, and the following day, the actors began losing their vision. Both became temporarily blind and were hospitalized in the same room for two weeks with their eyes bandaged. hey found they had a lot in common, and soon became fast friends. They remained so until Green died in the early '70s. Their sight returned after their hospital stay.

Colchis, the location of the Golden Fleece, is a real-life location on the east coast of the Black Sea, in western Georgia.

Goofs

Gen. Gavin is wearing a Senior Parachutist badge in 1944.The Parachutist Badge was formally approved on 10 March 1941. The senior and master parachutist's badges were authorized by Headquarters, Department of the Army, in 1949 and were announced by Change 4, Army Regulation 600-70, dated 24 January 1950.

When the ships are about to begin bombarding the beaches you see a group of planes fly by the camera. These are Douglas Sky Raiders, which did not see service until the late 1940s.

When the French first attack the casino there is barbed wire, but when they run from the hotel to the casino there is none.

In the opening battle scene, some of the streets appear wet with rain, while others are dry.

The Sword in the Stone. The kingdom of Britain has, for years, remained divided. Wart, a measly servant knave, dreams of becoming a knight but is barely certain he may act as squire to castle lord Sir Ector son Kay; then, the sorcerer Merlin and his grumpy, talking owl Archimedes invite themselves to the studio and move into the north tower.

Merlin, who can magically access the future, intends to prepare Wart for a grand future, so he gives the squirt dangerous lessons, transforming themselves into animals to learn the mental skills befitting a knight and a ruler. Since the once-renown magical sword in the stone that could confer the kingdom of all England unto one person (thus unifying it) has never been able to be withdrawn for years, a tournament in London is formed to designate a ruler instead. Kay is going to compete, but the rude, lout stands no chance.

Budget
$3,000,000 (estimated)

Run time 1h 19mins

Trivia

Arthur was voiced by three different boys - Rickie Sorensen, Richard Reitherman and Robert Reitherman. The changes in voice are very noticeable in the film because of the way Arthur's voice keeps going from broken to unbroken, sometimes in the same scene. One of the easiest noticed is in the last scene in the throne room when Arthur asks in his "changed voice", "Oh, Archimedes, I wish Merlin was here!" Then, the camera cuts farther back and Arthur shouts in his "unchanged voice," "Merlin! Merlin!"

Although Walt Disney never knew it, he himself was character designer Bill Peet's model for Merlin. Peet saw them both as argumentative, cantankerous, but playful and very intelligent. Peet also gave Merlin Walt's nose. This was the second instance in which Walt unknowingly served as model for a wizard, the first being the wizard Yensid from the Sorcerer's Apprentice in Fantasia (1940). This explains why the character was given the name Yensid. This read backwards is Disney.

Goofs

Throughout the entire film Wart's voice keeps on changing from being child-like to adult-like. One of the easiest spots to notice this is in the throne room towards the end when Wart is trying to get somebody else to take his place. He says "Oh Archimedes, I wish Merlin were here!" in his adult voice, then the camera goes to a distant view and he calls "Merlin, Merlin" in his child voice.

When Arthur as a squirrel falls on the broken tree branch after being pushed by the old lady squirrel, his mouth doesn't move the first time the yells "Help!"

When Pelinore enters the castle, he takes the glove off his left hand. When he's passing Wart, however, his right hand is the one that is bare. Immediately afterwards the bare hand switches back to his left.

When Merlin and Wart are fishes in the moat, a turtle is seen swimming around. Britain has no native turtles.

Lord of the Flies. After a plane crash in the ocean, a group of British students reach an island. The boy Ralph organizes the other kids, assigning responsibilities for each one. When the rebel Jack neglects the fire camp and they lose the chance to be seen by an airplane, the group split under the leadership of Jack. While Ralph rationalizes the survival procedures, Jack returns to the primitivism, using the fear for the unknown (in a metaphor to the religion) and hunger to control the other boys. His group starts hunting and chasing pigs, stealing the possession of Ralph's group and even killing people.

Budget
$250,000 (estimated)

Cannes Film Festival 1963
Nominee Palme d'Or Peter Brook

Run time 1h 32mins

Trivia

According to the filmmaker's commentary on the DVD version of this film (at 0:06:09), because of the loud noise from the sea and jungle on the beaches of the islands on which the movie was set, none of the dialogue could be recorded synchronously at the actual locations where the scenes were filmed. Instead, at the end of each day, the actors would be taken to a quiet location in the interior of the islands, where the dialogue for the scenes they had just filmed would be recorded from memory to be re-mixed, word by word, during the editing process. The one exception is the scene where Piggy tells some of the younger children how his hometown of Camberley got its name (which is also the only scene in the movie which is not based on a scene in the original book.)

During the first week of film shooting on the Island of Vieques, Puerto Rico, the Bay of Pigs Invasion began. This impacted filming because the wounded were evacuated to the U.S. naval hospital on Vieques.

Goofs

When Simon leaves the shelters on the beach, he is shirtless. Yet when he watches Jack and the hunters kill the pig, he is wearing a clean, white shirt. Later when we see Simon again, he is shirtless once again.

When first seen on the beach, the navy officer has no holster (with a gun inside), but having walked back to the landing craft he suddenly is then wearing it. (The book has him wearing it on the beach as a sign of his hypocrisy over violence by the boys).

As Piggy is near-sighted, his spectacles could not be used as a "magnifying glass" to light a bonfire: lenses for near-sightedness would scatter, not focus, the sun's rays. (This error occurs in the original novel and was perpetuated in the 1990 remake of the film.)

When Piggy's body is floating in the sea, the rope holding the doll near the rocks can be clearly seen.

MUSIC 1963

Artist	Single	Reached number one	Weeks at number one
1963			
Cliff Richard and The Shadows	"The Next Time" / "Bachelor Boy"	3rd January 1963	3
The Shadows	"Dance On!"	24th January 1963	1
Jet Harris and Tony Meehan	"Diamonds"	31st January 1963	3
Frank Ifield	"The Wayward Wind"	21st February 1963	3
Cliff Richard and The Shadows	"Summer Holiday"	14th March 1963	2
The Shadows	"Foot Tapper"	28th March 1963	1
Cliff Richard and The Shadows	"Summer Holiday"	4th April 1963	1
Gerry & The Pacemakers	"How Do You Do It?"	11th April 1963	3
The Beatles	"From Me to You"	2nd May 1963	7
Gerry & The Pacemakers	"I Like It"	20th June 1963	4
Frank Ifield	"Confessin' (That I Love You)"	18th July 1963	2
The Searchers	"Sweets for My Sweet"	8th August 1963	2
Billy J. Kramer & The Dakotas	"Bad to Me"	22nd August 1963	3
The Beatles	"She Loves You"	12th September 1963	4
Brian Poole and The Tremeloes	"Do You Love Me"	10th October 1963	3
Gerry & The Pacemakers	"You'll Never Walk Alone"	31st October 1963	4
The Beatles	"She Loves You"	28th November 1963	2
The Beatles	"I Want to Hold Your hand"	12th December 1963	5

The UK Singles Chart is the official record chart in the United Kingdom. Prior to 1969 there was no official singles chart; however, The Official Charts Company and Guinness' British Hit Singles & Albums regard the canonical sources as New Musical Express (NME) before 10th March 1960 and Record Retailer from then until 15th February 1969 when Retailer and the BBC jointly commissioned the British Market Research Bureau (BMRB) to compile the charts. The choice to use Record Retailer as the canonical source for the 1960s has been contentious because NME (which continued compiling charts beyond March 1960) had the biggest circulation of periodicals in the decade and was more widely followed. As well as the chart compilers mentioned previously, Melody Maker, Disc and Record Mirror all compiled their own charts during the decade. Due to the lack of any official chart the BBC aggregated results from all these charts to announce its own Pick of the Pops chart. One source explains that the reason for using the Record Retailer chart for the 1960s was that it was "the only chart to have as many as 50 positions for almost the entire decade". The sample size of Record Retailer in the early 1960s was around 30 stores whereas NME and Melody Maker were sampling over 100 stores. In 1969, the first BMRB chart was compiled using postal returns of sales logs from 250 record shops.

Cliff Richard and The Shadows

"The Next Time" / "Bachelor Boy"

"**Bachelor Boy**" is a song by Cliff Richard and the Shadows, written by Richard and Bruce Welch (from the Shadows). It became a hit when it was released as the B-side of Richard's single "The Next Time". Both sides of the single were regarded as having chart potential so both sides were promoted and, in many markets, "Bachelor Boy" became the bigger hit. The single spent three weeks at No. 1 in the UK Singles Chart in January 1963 and was a major hit internationally, although it only reached No. 99 in the US. Both sides of the single were included on the accompanying soundtrack album Summer Holiday. On the soundtrack album the Michael Sammes Singers were credited as backing singers, although they were not credited on the single.

The Shadows

"Dance On!"

"**Dance On!**" is an instrumental by British group the Shadows, released as a single in December 1962. It went to number 1 on the UK Singles Chart and the Irish Singles Chart. A vocal version, with lyrics by Marcel Stellman, was recorded by British female vocalist Kathy Kirby, whose version reached number 11 on the UK chart in September 1963.

"Dance On!" was written by Valerie Murtagh, Elaine Murtagh and Ray Adams, better known for being the members of pop vocal group the Avons. It was released with the B-side "All Day", written by Bruce Welch and Hank Marvin. In the US and Canada, "Dance On!" was released with the B-side "The Rumble", written by guitarist Ike Isaacs.

Jet Harris and Tony Meehan

"Diamonds"

"Diamonds" is an instrumental composed by Jerry Lordan and first released as a single by Jet Harris and Tony Meehan in January 1963. It became a number-one hit on the UK Singles Chart, spending three weeks at the top of the chart. In 1962, guitarist Jet Harris left the Shadows and was signed to Decca Records as a solo artist, releasing his debut hit single "Besame Muscho" in May 1962. Former Shadows' drummer Tony Meehan was working at Decca as a producer and suggested to Harris that they team up. He asked Jerry Lordan, writer of several hits for the Shadows ("Apache", "Wonderful Land" and "Atlantis"), for an instrumental with bass guitar and a drum solo, and he gave them "Diamonds".

"Diamonds" was recorded on 23 November 1962 at Decca Studios.

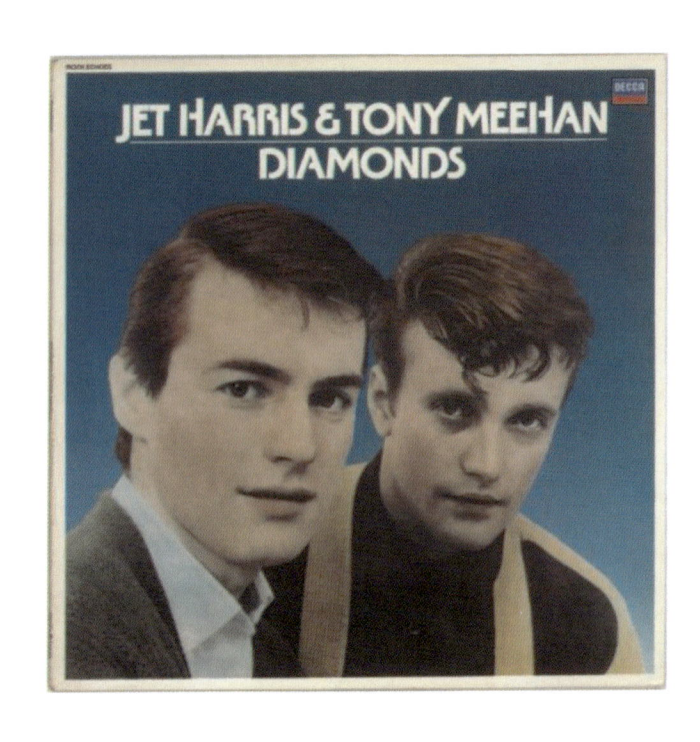

Frank Ifield

"The Wayward Wind"

"The Wayward Wind" is a country song written by Stanley Lebowsky (music) and Herb Newman (lyrics).

Members of the Western Writers of America chose the song as one of the Top 100 Western songs of all time.

The "Wayward Wind" of the title is a metaphor for wanderlust: an irrepressible urge to travel and explore. This is further emphasized by describing it as a "restless wind." In the context of the 19th century setting of shanty towns and railroads, the Western United States was still largely unexplored by European settlers. Concurrent to the era of lone cowboys on horseback, the First transcontinental railroad was built. Steam trains were a gateway the American frontier romanticized in literature, songs and film.

Cliff Richard and The Shadows

"Summer Holiday"

"Summer Holiday" is a song recorded by Cliff Richard and The Shadows, written by rhythm guitarist Bruce Welch and drummer Brian Bennett. It is taken from the film of the same name, and was released as the second single from the film in February 1963. It went to number one in the UK Singles Chart for a total of two weeks, after "Summer Holiday" had spent two weeks at number one, The Shadows' instrumental "Foot Tapper"—also from the same film—took over the top spot for one week, before "Summer Holiday" returned to the top spot for one further week.

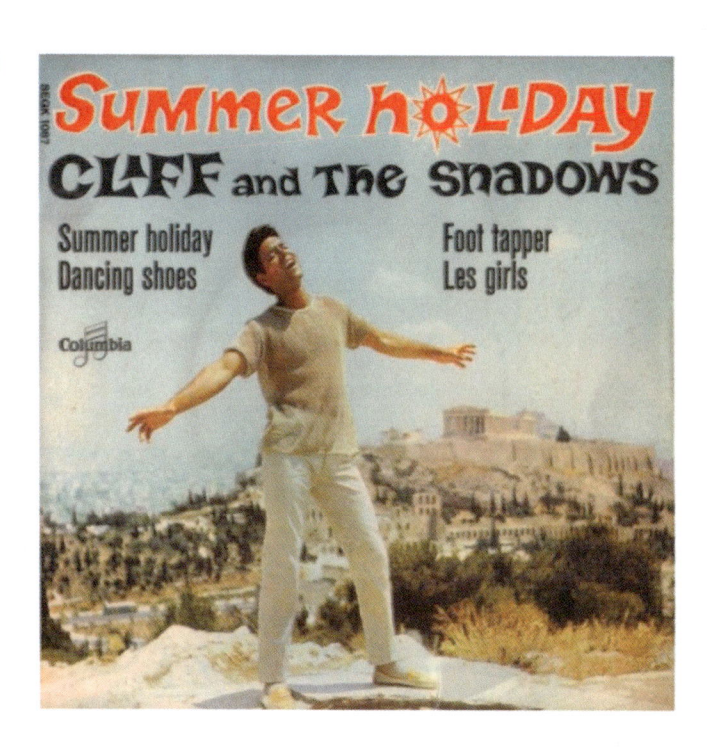

The track is one of Richard's best-known titles and it remains a staple of his live shows. It was one of six hits Richard performed at his spontaneous gig at the 1996 Wimbledon Championships when rain stopped the tennis.

The Shadows

"Foot Tapper"

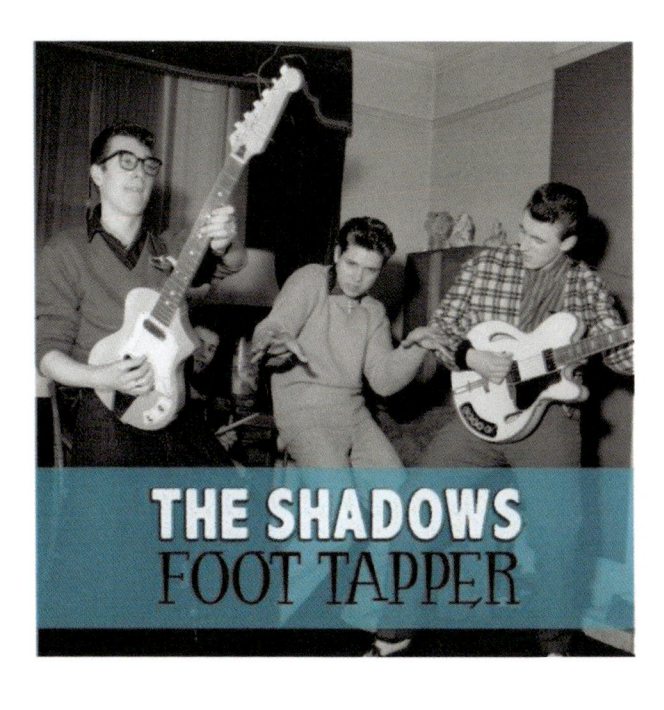

"Foot Tapper" is an instrumental by British guitar group the Shadows, released as a single in February 1963. It went to number one in the UK Singles Chart, and was the Shadows' last UK number-one hit (not including those where they performed as Cliff Richard's backing group). Reviewed in New Record Mirror, it was described as "a beautifully balanced bit of recording with a compelling theme. Hank, Licorice and Bruce are in precise, driving form – but the side showcases Brian's forceful but controlled drumming, notably on cymbals. Just try and stop your foot tapping. It'll fair hurtle into the charts – and is probably even better than "Dance On". Reviewing for Disc, Don Nicholl described "Foot Tapper" as a "light-hearted modern dancer which will pull in as many customers as the other side – maybe more".

Gerry and the Pacemakers.

"How Do You Do It?"

"How Do You Do It?" was the debut single by Liverpudlian band Gerry and the Pacemakers. It was written by Mitch Murray. The song reached number one in the UK Singles Chart on 11th April 1963, where it stayed for three weeks. The song was written by Mitch Murray, who offered it to Adam Faith and Brian Poole but was turned down. George Martin of EMI, feeling the song had enormous hit potential, decided to pick it up for the new group he was producing, the Beatles, as the A-side of their first single. The Beatles recorded the song on 4 September 1962 with Ringo Starr on drums. The group was initially opposed to recording it, feeling that it did not fit their sound.

Gerry and the Pacemakers' version of "How Do You Do It?" was initially issued in the US and Canada in the spring of 1963, but made no impact on the charts.

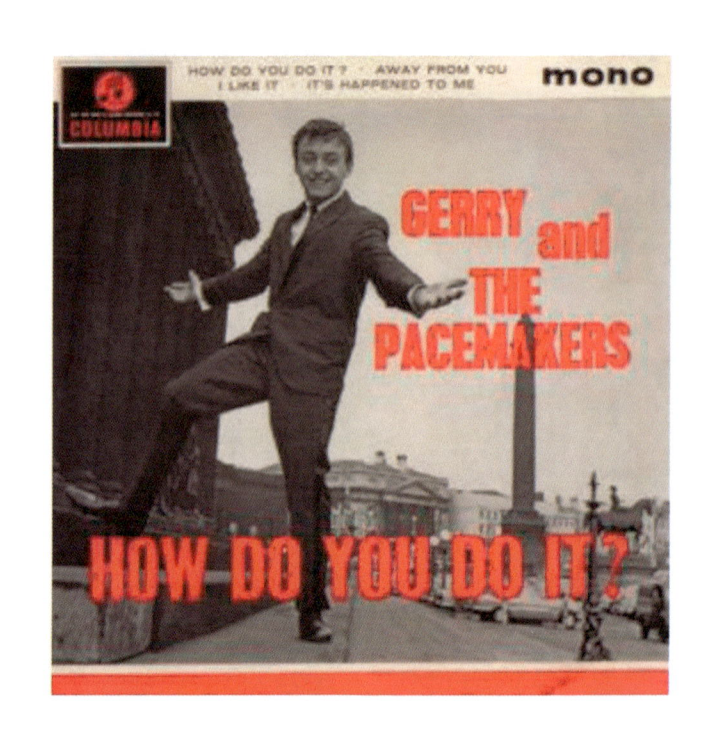

The Beatles

"From Me to You"

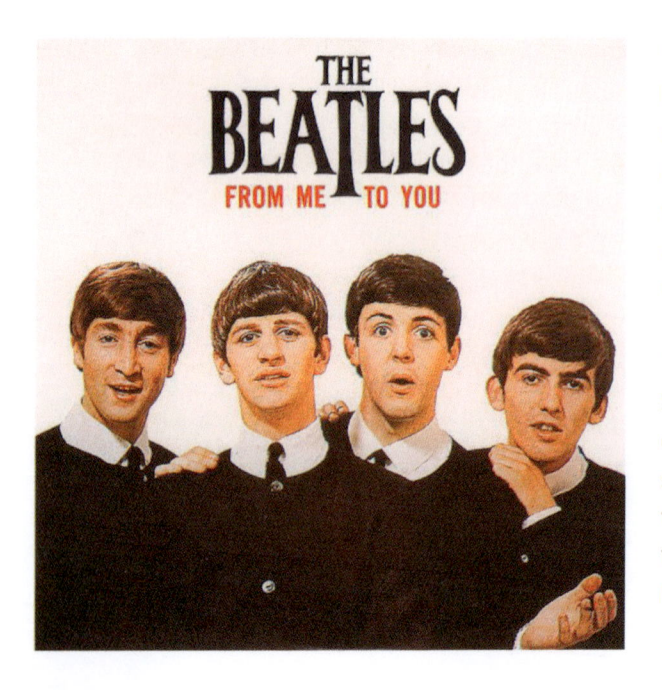

"From Me to You" is a song by the English rock band the Beatles that was released in April 1963 as their third single. It was written by Paul McCartney and John Lennon. The song was the Beatles' first number 1 hit on what became the official UK singles chart but the second, after "Please Please Me", on most of the other singles charts published in the UK at the time.

"From Me to You" failed to make an impact in the United States at the time of its initial release. Instead, a 1963 cover version released by Del Shannon resulted in the song becoming the first Lennon–McCartney tune to enter the US pop charts. The Beatles' original was rereleased in the US in January 1964 as the B-side to "Please Please Me", and reached number 41.

Gerry and the Pacemakers

"I Like It"

"I Like It" is the second single by Liverpudlian band Gerry and the Pacemakers. Like Gerry Marsden's first number one "How Do You Do It", it was written by Mitch Murray.

The song reached number one in the UK Singles Chart on 20th June 1963, where it stayed for four weeks. It reached No. 17 in the American charts in 1964. Cash Box described it as "a happy-go-lucky jumper that Gerry solo vocals in ear-arresting style."

It was used in the first part of two-part Australian miniseries called Peter Allen: Not the Boy Next Door that screened in 2015 on Channel Seven. A cover version of the song, sung by a child, was used in a Petits Filous advert in the late 1990s.

Frank Ifield

"Confessin"

"(I'm) Confessin' (that I Love You)" is a jazz and popular standard that has been recorded many times.

The song was first produced with different lyrics as "Lookin' For Another Sweetie", credited to Chris Smith and Sterling Grant, and recorded by Thomas "Fats" Waller & His Babies on 18th December 1929.

In 1930 it was reborn as "Confessin'", with new lyrics by Al Neiburg, and with the music this time credited to Doc Daugherty and Ellis Reynolds. Louis Armstrong made his first, and highly influential, recording of the song in August 1930, and continued to play it throughout his career. Unlike the crooners, Armstrong did not try to deliver the original song's lyrics or melody; instead, he smeared and dropped lyrics and added melodic scat breaks.

Elvis Presley

"(You're the) Devil in Disguise"

"(You're the) Devil in Disguise" is a 1963 single by Elvis Presley which was written by Bill Giant, Bernie Baum and Florence Kaye. It was published by Elvis Presley Music in June 1963.

The song peaked at No. 3 in the US on the Billboard singles chart on August 10, 1963 and No. 9 on the Billboard Rhythm and Blues singles chart, becoming his last top ten single on the Rhythm and Blues charts. The single was certified "Gold" by the RIAA for sales in excess of 500,000 units in the US. The song also topped Japan's Utamatic record chart in the fall of 1963. In 1963, when the song was debuted to a British audience on the BBC television show Juke Box Jury, celebrity guest John Lennon voted the song "a miss" stating on the new song that Elvis Presley was "like Bing Crosby now". The song went on to reach No. 1 in the UK for a single week.

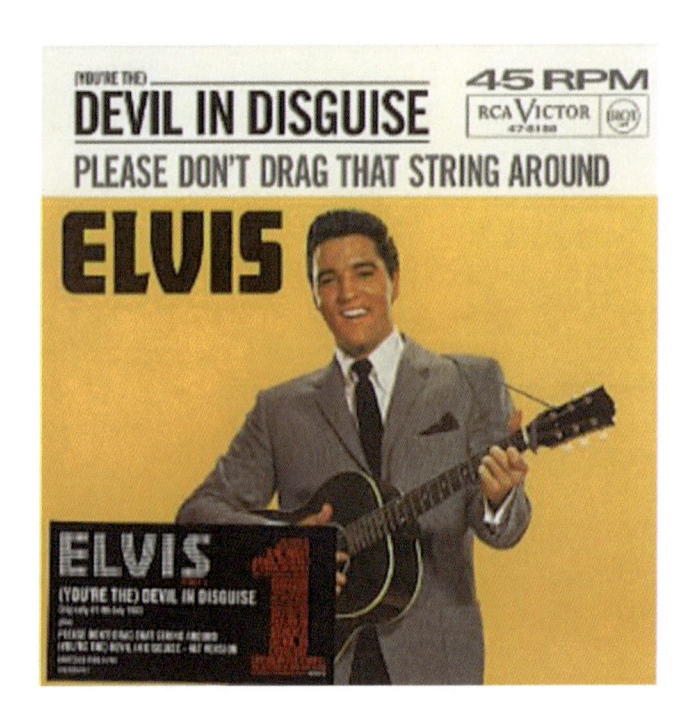

The Searchers

"Sweets for my Sweets"

"Sweets for My Sweet" In 1963, "Sweets for My Sweet" was released by Merseybeat band the Searchers as their debut single, reaching No. 1 on the UK Single Chart for two weeks that August. The Searchers' version was also issued in the US in 1964 but failed to chart. Pan-European magazine Music & Media wrote, "The Searchers 1963 classic is completely reworked in a dead trendy ragga version, which is so cheerful that you can't believe storms and depression ever existed. Nobody will be surprised that it's heavily played on Bay Radio/St. Julian's on holiday island Malta." Alan Jones from Music Week said, "Yes, it is the old Searchers hit, and it sounds surprisingly good too considering it has been dragged uncompromisingly into the Nineties. Now an easy to swallow confection, part reggae, part jack swing, it slips down a treat."

Billy J Kramer and The Dakotas

"Bad to Me"

"Bad to Me" is a song credited to Lennon–McCartney. In late interviews, John Lennon said that he wrote it for Billy J. Kramer with The Dakotas while on holiday in Spain. However, in a 1964 interview he said that he and Paul McCartney wrote it in the back of a van, declaring McCartney a contributor. Bootlegs exist of Lennon's original demo of the song, which was recorded on 31 May 1963.

An acoustic demo from the same era was released on iTunes in December 2013 on the album The Beatles Bootleg Recordings 1963. It became one of the first occasions a Lennon–McCartney composition made the US Top 40 recorded by an artist other than the Beatles (the first being "A World Without Love" by Peter & Gordon; another being "Goodbye" by Mary Hopkin).

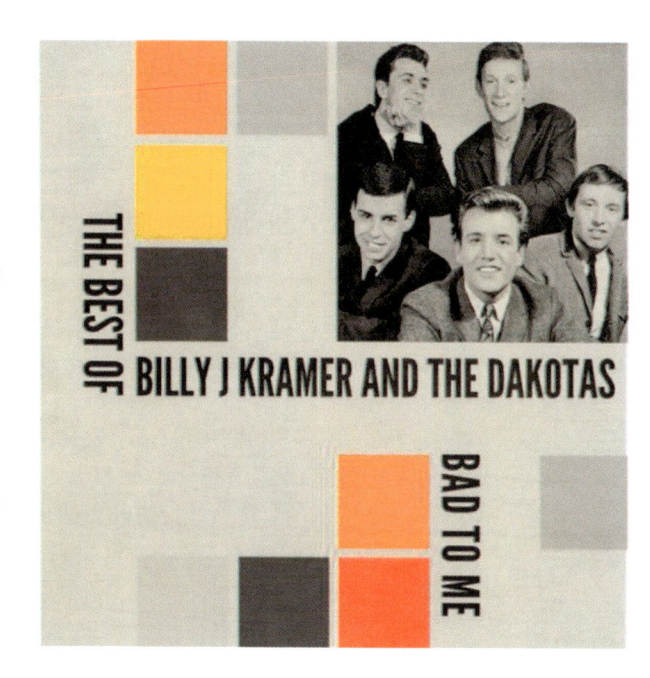

The Beatles

"She Loves You"

"She Loves You" is a song written by John Lennon and Paul McCartney and recorded by English rock band the Beatles for release as a single in 1963. The single set and surpassed several sales records in the United Kingdom charts, and set a record in the United States as one of the five Beatles songs that held the top five positions in the charts simultaneously, on 4th April 1964. It remains the band's best-selling single in the United Kingdom and the top-selling single of the 1960s there by any artist. In November 2004, Rolling Stone ranked "She Loves You" number 64 on their list of the 500 Greatest Songs of All Time. In August 2009, at the end of its "Beatles Weekend", BBC Radio 2 announced that "She Loves You" was the Beatles' all-time best-selling single in the UK based on information compiled by the Official Charts Company.

Gerry and the Pacemakers

"You'll Never Walk Alone"

"**You'll Never Walk Alone**" is a show tune from the 1945 Rodgers and Hammerstein musical *Carousel*. In the second act of the musical, Nettie Fowler, the cousin of the protagonist Julie Jordan, sings "You'll Never Walk Alone" to comfort and encourage Julie when her husband, Billy Bigelow, the male lead, accidentally falls on to his knife whilst trying to run away after attempting a robbery. The song is also sung at association football clubs around the world, where it is performed by a massed chorus of supporters on match day; this tradition developed at Liverpool F.C. after the chart success of the 1963 single of the song by the local Liverpool group Gerry and the Pacemakers. In some areas of the UK and Europe, "You'll Never Walk Alone" became the anthem of support for medical staff, first responders, and those in quarantine during the COVID-19 pandemic.

The Beatles

"I Want to Hold Your Hand"

"**I Want to Hold Your Hand**" is a song by the English rock band the Beatles. Written by John Lennon and Paul McCartney, and recorded on 17th October 1963, it was the first Beatles record to be made using four-track equipment. With advance orders exceeding one million copies in the United Kingdom, "I Want to Hold Your Hand" would have gone straight to the top of the British record charts on its day of release (29 November 1963) had it not been blocked by the group's first million-seller "She Loves You", their previous UK single, which was having a resurgence of popularity following intense media coverage of the group. Taking two weeks to dislodge its predecessor, "I Want to Hold Your Hand" stayed at number one for five weeks and remained in the UK top 50 for 21 weeks in total.

WORLD EVENTS 1963

January

1st — The #1 ranked (and unofficial college football champion) USC Trojans and the #2 Wisconsin Badgers met in the 1963 Rose Bowl before a crowd of 98,696 people. At the time, American college football's national championship was determined by the AP and UPI polls taken at the end of the regular season. The nation's first and second ranked teams happened to meet by virtue of being the respective champions of the Big Six Conference (now the Pac-12 Conference) and the Big Ten Conference. USC won 42-37, holding off a fourth quarter, 23-point rally by Wisconsin.

2nd — The Battle of Ap Bac in South Vietnam began, and was the first time that Viet Cong forces stood and fought against a major South Vietnamese attack. At the outset, Viet Cong ground fire shot down a United States Army UH-1 attack helicopter and four U.S. Army CH-21 transport helicopters as they arrived at their landing zone. Republic of Vietnam Air Force C-123 Provider transport planes dropped about 300 South Vietnamese paratroopers later in the day. Despite outnumbering the Viet Cong 4 to 1, and having American armour, artillery and helicopters, "what should have been an ARVN victory turned into an exercise of everything that was wrong with the South Vietnamese army".

3rd — Thirty-two Soviet civilians, from Siberia, forced their way into the United States Embassy in Moscow, describing themselves as "persecuted Christians" and seeking political asylum. After embassy officials told the group that they could not stay, the people were placed on a bus and taken away by Moscow police. The 6 men, 12 women and 14 children were sent back to Chernogorsk that evening, after the U.S. Embassy received assurances that the group would get "good treatment".

7th — The price of a mailing a letter in the United States rose from four cents to five cents, with a 25% increase in the price of a first-class stamp. The increase was the first since 1st August 1958, when the price had changed from three cents to four.

8th — Leonardo da Vinci's Mona Lisa was exhibited in the United States for the first time, at the National Gallery of Art in Washington, D.C., in an event attended by President Kennedy and 2,000 other guests of honour. The masterpiece was on view for 27 days in Washington, during which 674,000 visitors came to see it, then moved on to the Metropolitan Museum of Art in New York from 6th February to 4th March.

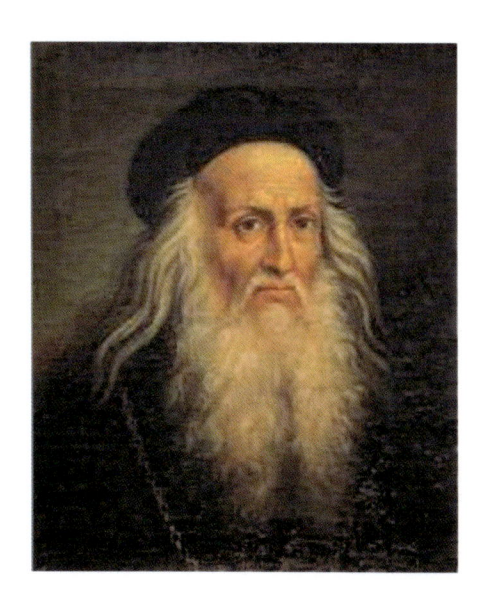

January

11th Two people in China, an 18-year-old fisherman and his seven-year-old younger brother, were fatally injured after the man took home a piece of radioactive cobalt-60 that had been dropped on farmland owned by the Anhui Agricultural University in Hefei. The cobalt-60 radiation was 43 petabecquerel; over a period of almost nine days before the sample was recovered, the man was exposed to 806 grays of radiation and died on 23rd January; his brother died two days later from exposure to 40 grays.

12th At the Australian National Athletics Championships in her home town of Perth, Western Australia, Margaret Burvill set a new world record of 23.2 seconds in the women's 220-yard dash.

14th The locomotive Flying Scotsman (British Railways No. 60103) made its last scheduled run, before going into the hands of Alan Pegler for preservation.

16th Soviet Premier Nikita Khrushchev made a visit to the Berlin Wall from the East Berlin side, then delivered an address to the Communist leadership of East Germany at the SED Party Congress. Khrushchev stated bluntly that the Wall had accomplished its purpose of stemming the exodus of citizens from the nation and stabilized the East German economy, and added that further Soviet economic assistance would not be forthcoming. "Neither God nor the devil will give you bread or butter if you do not manage it with your own hands," Khrushchev said, adding that East Germany "must not expect alms from some rich uncle".

18th The French automobile manufacturer Simca was taken over by the American automaker Chrysler, which purchased a controlling interest of the 18,000-employee company in order to increase its presence in Europe.

January

19th — Hermine Braunsteiner, formerly a supervising warden at the Ravensbrück concentration camp, and known as "The Stomping Mare" because of her use of steel-studded jackboots to kick inmates, became a naturalized citizen of the United States. Acting on a tip from Nazi hunter Simon Wiesenthal, the New York Times would expose her past in 1964. Her citizenship would be revoked in 1971, and in 1973 she would be extradited to West Germany for trial as a war criminal. In 1981, she would be sentenced to life imprisonment. Released after 15 years for health reasons (including, ironically, the amputation of her leg), she would die in 1999.

22nd — In Paris, President Charles de Gaulle of France and Chancellor Konrad Adenauer of West Germany signed the Elysée Treaty, the first bilateral pact between the French and German nations. "In the century prior to the treaty", it would be observed later, "France and Germany had been on opposite sides in three wars: the Franco-Prussian War, World War I and World War II." The treaty provided for the nations' leaders to meet at least twice a year, and the foreign and defence ministers to meet four times a year.

23rd — Three months after the U.S. and the U.S.S.R. almost went to war during the Cuban Missile Crisis, the Turkish government announced the deactivation and removal of its arsenal of American-supplied Jupiter missiles from Turkey, six days after Italy had announced their phaseout of the Jupiters. The missiles in Turkey, armed with nuclear warheads and within striking distance of cities in the Soviet Union, had been one of the reasons for the Soviet placement of missiles in Cuba.

24th — A B-52C bomber, carrying two nuclear weapons and on airborne alert for the U.S. Air Force, lost its vertical stabilizer in turbulence, broke up in mid-air and crashed into Elephant Mountain in Piscataquis County, Maine. Seven of the nine-man crew were killed, and one of the unarmed nuclear bombs fell from the plane and broke apart on impact on a farm. A part of that bomb, containing enriched uranium, was never located, "even though the waterlogged farmland in the vicinity was excavated to a depth of 50 feet".

25th — A large annular solar eclipse covered over 99% of the Sun, creating a dramatic spectacle for observers in a narrow path at most 19.6 km wide; it lasted just 25.24 seconds at the point of maximum eclipse.

26th — The "British Pools Panel" was first used to address instances, in the betting on Britain's soccer football matches, where a scheduled match was postponed. On the first weekend, when 55 games were called off because of freezing temperatures, the panel of former players and referees "predicted" what the results would have been had the match not been postponed, essentially making up results that would be accepted for determining whether a betting line had been picked successfully. Originally, the five-member Panel only intervened if 30 or more matches were called off; later, the panel would convene if any match were postponed.

27th — Lee Harvey Oswald used the alias "A. J. Hidell" for the first time, ordering a .38 caliber Smith & Wesson revolver through the mail from Seaport Traders, Inc., of Los Angeles. He would use the Hidell name in ordering other weapons, including the Mannlicher–Carcano rifle that would be used in November to kill U.S. President Kennedy.

31st — Major General H. W. G. Wijeyekoon left office as Commander of the Ceylon Army.

February

1st	Middle East Airlines Flight 265, with 14 people on board, was struck by a Turkish Air Force C-47 airplane with 3 people, as the airliner was descending for a landing at the airport in Ankara. Plunging from an altitude of 7,000 feet, the wreckage of Flight 265 fell into Ulas Square, killing another 87 people and injuring 200.
2nd	The world record for the pole vault was broken by Pentti Nikula of Finland, after having been held by a succession of Americans for almost 35 years. Nikula cleared the bar at 4.94 meters (16 feet, 8+3/4 inches) using a fiberglass pole.
4th	The SS Marine Sulphur Queen, a tanker with a crew of 39 and a cargo of molten sulphur, was heard from for the last time, two days after its departure from Beaumont, Texas en route to Norfolk, Virginia. Contact between the ship and its owner, Marine Transport Lines, Inc., was lost and the ship was reported missing two days later. Debris from the tanker washed ashore in Florida, but a search by U.S. Coast Guard and U.S. Navy airplanes did not locate the ship. The story of the disappearance of the tanker would first be described as a casualty of the "Bermuda Triangle" in the Argosy magazine article "The Deadly Bermuda Triangle", although an investigating panel concluded that the ship, structurally unsound and burdened by its heavy cargo, broke in half during a storm.
7th	In one of New Zealand's worst road accidents ever, a bus crashed after its brakes failed nearing the top of the southern descent of the Brynderwyn Range, killing 15 of the 35 people on board. The bus, bringing back a group of Maori people from a welcome for Queen Elizabeth's visit to Waitangi, plunged over a 130-foot embankment, and evoked memories of a December 24, 1953, train crash that killed 151 people who were on their way to Auckland to welcome the Queen to New Zealand.
10th	Five Japanese cities located on the northernmost part of Kyūshū were merged to become the city of Kitakyūshū, with a population of more than one million.
11th	The CIA's Domestic Operations Division was created. Aerial view of the Central Intelligence Agency headquarters, Langley, Virginia.
14th	The Coca-Cola Company introduced its first low calorie soft drink, TaB, test marketing it in Springfield, Massachusetts.
15th	Television was introduced in Singapore, with one hour per week of programming initially, increasing by April to five hours of programming each weeknight, and 10 hours each on Saturday and Sunday.

February

17th	Turkey accepted the proposal to remove the remaining Jupiter nuclear missiles based there by the United States, with the last of the weapons taken out by 24th April; nuclear defence of Turkey would be replaced by Polaris submarines.
18th	Mount Agung, a dormant volcano on the Indonesian island of Bali, became active again for the first time in 120 years. Its lava flow would destroy villages in the vicinity and kill more than 1,000 people.
21st	Telstar 1, the first privately financed satellite, became the first satellite to be destroyed by radiation. Telstar had been launched from the United States eight months earlier on 10th July 1962, one day after the U.S. had conducted a high-altitude nuclear test, and the increased concentration of electrons in the Van Allen radiation belt had caused the communication satellite's transponders to deteriorate.
22nd	The fictional cartoon character Pebbles Flintstone was "born" in an episode of the cartoon The Flintstones called "The Blessed Event".
24th	Jonny Nilsson won the 10,000m speed skating event to win the World All-round Speed Skating Championships in Japan, with Knut Johannesen second and Nils Aaness third.
25th	An unnamed ferry collided with a Japanese cargo ship off Kobe and sank. Of the 64 people on board, nineteen were rescued, seven killed and 38 reported missing.
26th	A final piece of debris from the decaying orbit of Mars 2MV-4 No.1 re-entered the earth's atmosphere.
27th	Juan Bosch took office as the 41st president of the Dominican Republic. His democratically elected government would exist for less than seven months, and be overthrown by a military coup on 25th September 1963.
28th	Dorothy Schiff resigned from the New York Newspaper Publishers Association, saying that the city needed at least one paper operating during the newspaper strike. Her newspaper, the New York Post, would resume publication on 4th March.

March

1st — Eurocontrol, the European Organisation for the Safety of Air Navigation, came into existence as an international treaty signed on 13th December 1960, by West Germany, France, the United Kingdom, Belgium, Netherlands and Luxembourg became effective.

2nd — The first attempt at liver transplantation in a human being was made by a team in Denver, led by Dr. Thomas Starzl. The patient, an unidentified 3-year-old child, died shortly after the surgery. On 23rd July 1967, Dr. Starzl would perform the first liver transplant where a patient survived for longer than one year.

4th — In Paris, six people were sentenced to death for conspiring to assassinate President Charles de Gaulle. Three of the men— Georges Watin, Serge Bernier and Lajos Marton— had eluded capture and were tried, convicted and sentenced in absentia. Lt. Col. Jean-Marie Bastien-Thiry, Lt. Alain de Bougernet, and Jacques Prevost were put on death row. De Gaulle would pardon all but Bastien-Thiry, who would be executed by firing squad on 11th March.

5th — In Camden, Tennessee, country music superstar Patsy Cline (Virginia Patterson Hensley) was killed in a plane crash along with fellow performers and Cline's manager and pilot Randy Hughes, while returning from a benefit performance in Kansas City, Kansas, for country radio disc jockey "Cactus" Jack Call.

7th — The 58-story tall Pan Am Building (now the MetLife Building) opened at 200 Park Avenue in New York City. With more than three million square feet of floor space, it was the largest commercial office building in the world at the time of its completion.

10th — The first air show for the "Confederate Air Force", a group dedicated to preserving World War II aircraft, took place, in Texas. The organization was renamed the Commemorative Air Force in later years.

12th — Lee Harvey Oswald, using the name of "A. Hidell", mailed a money order in the amount of $21.45 to Klein's Sporting Goods of Chicago, along with a coupon clipped from the February 1963 issue of American Rifleman magazine, to purchase a rifle that would be used eight months later to kill President John F. Kennedy.

13th — Up and coming heavyweight boxer Cassius Clay almost had his career derailed in a bout at New York City's Madison Square Garden, against Doug Jones. Although the future Muhammad Ali, had predicted he would defeat Jones in four rounds, Clay appeared to be losing the bout as it went into round 7. Scheduled for only ten rounds, the fight ended in a decision in favour of Clay, with many in the crowd protesting that it had been fixed. Clay would win the right to face Sonny Liston the following year, and win the title.

15th — The first confirmed penetration of United States airspace by Soviet military aircraft took place with two violations on the same day over the state of Alaska. One Soviet reconnaissance plane flew over Nelson Island, while the other made a pass over Nunivak Island.

19th — The 89-year-old ship SS Arctic Bear, which had served in the United States Coast Guard and the navy of Canada, and had assisted the Antarctic exploration by Admiral Richard E. Byrd, was being towed from Nova Scotia to Philadelphia, where it was to be used as a floating restaurant. En route, the Bear ran into a storm and sank

March

21st — The Alcatraz Island federal penitentiary in San Francisco Bay closed because it cost twice as much to operate as other units in the federal system. The last 27 prisoners were transferred elsewhere at the order of Attorney General Robert F. Kennedy. Frank P. Weatherman was the last of the 27 inmates to depart the prison.

23rd — Microbiologist Maurice Hilleman, who would develop nearly 40 vaccines, including eight of the 14 on the worldwide vaccination schedule, began the development of the Mumpsvax vaccine against the mumps virus, by harvesting the live virus from his five-year-old daughter. The strain of mumps virus that was used to develop the vaccine was given the name "Jeryl Lynn" after the little girl, Jeryl Lynn Hilleman.

25th — Pilot Ralph Flores and his passenger, Helen Klaben, were rescued, 49 days after their plane crashed in northern British Columbia. On 4th February, Flores and Klaben had disappeared on their way back to the United States, and survived in sub-zero temperatures with almost no food for seven weeks. The story was made into the film Hey, I'm Alive, with Edward Asner and Sally Struthers portraying the two survivors.

27th — Grigori Nelyubov, Ivan Anikeyev and Valentin Filatyev, three of the original 20 cosmonauts selected for the Soviet space program, ended their careers when they got drunk and then got into an argument with military guards at the Chkalovskaya subway station in Moscow. Rather than making it into outer space, all three were dismissed from the program.

28th — Four women in Kankakee, Illinois, claimed that they were dealt four perfect bridge hands, with the dealer getting all 13 spades in her 13 playing cards, her partner having 13 diamonds, and the other two players having 13 hearts and 13 clubs. According to a probability expert, the odds were "2,554,511,322,166,132,992,844,640,000 to one" against the event. On 22nd October, a group of women in Jacksonville, Florida, would report being dealt four perfect hands and a group of women in Fort Lauderdale, Florida would report the same incident on 27th January 1964. The Guinness Book of World Records has noted that "if all the people in the world were grouped in bridge fours, and each four were dealt 120 hands a day, it would require 62 x 1012 years before one 'perfect' deal could be expected to recur."

29th — A bolt of lightning struck the nose of a TWA Boeing 707 shortly after it took off a flight from London to New York, and tore a 21-inch by 8-inch hole in the fuselage. The TWA pilot jettisoned 10,000 gallons of fuel while circling for 35 minutes over southwestern England before safely landing at London with his 110 passengers, who included 22 Methodist ministers on their way home from a tour of Israel, MGM Films President Robert O'Brien, and film actor Warren Beatty.

30th — The first direct dialled trans-Atlantic telephone calls were made between the United Kingdom and the United States, through switching stations at London and White Plains, New York.

31st — A military coup in Guatemala overthrew the government of President Miguel Ydígoras Fuentes, who was flown to exile in Nicaragua after the takeover by his Defence Minister, Colonel Enrique Peralta Azurdia. The coup took place after Juan José Arévalo, a Communist supporter and former President, returned to Guatemala and announced that he would run in the November presidential election. Ex-President Ydígoras, who had believed that Arévalo had a good chance of winning the race, told reporters the next day, "What is going on in Guatemala is for her own good and for the good of the rest of Central America." Peralta would remain in power until 1966.

April

1st — The long-running American TV soap opera General Hospital made its début on the ABC network. On the same afternoon, the first episode of NBC's hospital soap opera, The Doctors premiered. General Hospital, set in the fictional town of Port Charles, New York, would begin its 50th year in 2012, while The Doctors, set in the fictional New England town of Madison, would end on 31st December 1982.

3rd — The Delaware Supreme Court upheld their state's law, unique in the United States, permitting the flogging of criminals. Although the penalty, dating from colonial days, had not been carried out for several years, a 20-year-old man had been given a probated sentence of 20 lashes for auto theft, then violated the probation.

4th — The cost of making a long-distance telephone call was lowered throughout the continental United States, with a maximum charge of one dollar for three-minute "station-to-station" calls made between 9:00 pm and 4:30 a.m. The equivalent 50 years later for a 1963 dollar would be $7.50.

5th — The Soviet Union accepted an American proposal to establish a Moscow–Washington hotline so that the leaders of the two nations could communicate directly with each other in order to avoid war. Originally, the hot line was a teletype system rather than a direct voice line.

6th — The South African Soccer League, formed in 1961, was banned from further use of public stadiums because its teams included white, black and mixed-race players, in violation of the Group Areas Act, and a game at Alberton, a suburb of Johannesburg, was cancelled on the day of the match. Fans climbed the fence surrounding the locked Natalspruit Indian Sports ground and 15,000 people watched the Moroka Swallows defeat Blackpool United, 6–1. Afterwards, the SASL was permanently denied access to playing fields, and disbanded in 1967 after years of financial losses.

7th — At more than 700 pages, the first full Sunday edition of the New York Times since the end of the printer's strike set a record for the size of a newspaper. The Times edition weighed seven and a half pounds.

10th — The U.S. nuclear submarine Thresher sank during sea trials 220 miles (350 km) east of Cape Cod, killing the 112 U.S. Navy personnel and 17 civilians on board. The wreckage of Thresher would be located on 1st October 1964.

April

12th	The Soviet nuclear-powered submarine K-33 collided with the Finnish merchant vessel M/S Finn clipper in the Danish Straits. Although severely damaged, both vessels made it to port.
13th	The wreckage of the Dutch ship Vergulde Draeck was discovered almost 307 years after it sank off of the coast of Australia. The vessel, carrying 193 people, had gone down on 28th April 1656, with 118 drowning. Three centuries later, it was found by a group of skin-divers seven miles from Ledge Point, Western Australia.
15th	An unidentified 58-year-old man, suffering from lung cancer, was admitted to the University of Mississippi hospital. On 11th June 1963, he would become the first person to receive a lung transplant.
17th	Representatives of Egypt, Syria and Iraq signed a declaration in Cairo to merge their three nations into a new United Arab Republic. Egypt and Syria had been merged as the United Arab Republic from 1958 to 1961 before Syria withdrew, and Egypt and retained the UAR name. Demonstrations followed in Jordan, where citizens of the Kingdom wanted to join the federation, which was never ratified.
19th	Under pressure from the United States, South Korea's President Park Chung Hee returned to his pledge to return to civilian rule, and announced that multiparty elections for the presidency and the National Assembly would take place before the end of the year. Park had promised a return to democracy in 1963 when he had taken power in a coup on 12th August 1961, but on 16th March 1963, proposed to extend military rule for another four years. The voting (in which Park would be elected president) would be held on 15th October.
20th	In Montreal, the terrorist campaign of the Front de libération du Québec claimed its first fatality. William Vincent O'Neill, a 65-year-old night watchman and janitor, died in the explosion of a bomb at a Canadian Army recruitment centre. O'Neill, who was planning to retire at the end of May, had been scheduled to start his shift at midnight, but had arrived at 11:30 to allow a co-worker to go home, and was killed when the bomb exploded at 11:45 pm.
22nd	Cuba released its last American prisoners, 27 men who had been incarcerated by the Castro government. Twenty-one were flown from Havana to Miami after New York lawyer James Donovan had negotiated their freedom. Another six elected to go to other nations rather than returning to the U.S.
23rd	The Ukrainian football club FC Karpaty Lviv played its first official match, defeating Lokomotiv Gomel 1–0.
25th	The United States removed the last of its Jupiter missiles from Turkey, completing an agreement that had been reached with the Soviet Union after the Cuban Missile Crisis of 1962.
27th	The U.S. Marine Corps lost its first aircraft to enemy action in Vietnam, when a UH-34D transport helicopter was shot down by Viet Cong ground fire near Do Xa, South Vietnam.
30th	New Hampshire became the first of the United States to legalize a state lottery in the 20th century. The first drawing in the New Hampshire Sweepstakes would take place on 12th March 1964.

May

1st — American mountaineer Jim Whittaker and Sherpa guide Nawang Gombu became the fifth and sixth persons to successfully reach the top of Mount Everest, following Edmund Hillary and Tenzing Norgay (29th May 1953), and Ernst Reiss and Fritz Luchsinger (18th May 1957). Whittaker, a 32-year-old resident of Redmond, Washington, became the first American to accomplish the feat.

4th — The sinking of a motor launch on the Nile River drowned more than 185 people in Egypt, nearly all of them Moslem pilgrims who were beginning the journey to Mecca from the city of Maghagha. The boat's capacity was only 80 people, but more than 200 people crowded on board to make the trip. Among the 15 people who survived were the boat's captain, its owner and its conductor, who were all jailed while the matter was investigated.

5th — Graduate student Beverly Samans, 23, became the tenth murder victim of Albert DeSalvo. Unlike the first nine Boston Strangler victims, Samans was stabbed repeatedly, although he repeated his modus operandi of strangling a woman with her own stocking. Her body was discovered three days later.

7th — The communications satellite Telstar II was launched into Earth orbit to replace the first Telstar satellite, which had stopped functioning on 21st February because of damage by the Van Allen radiation belts. As with the first Telstar, the satellite amplified the signals that it was receiving from ground station transmitters.

May

9th — After the first six attempts at a successful launch of the MIDAS (Missile Defence Alarm System) satellite failed, MIDAS 7 was successfully placed into a polar orbit. During the first three years of attempts, three of the satellites failed to reach orbit, while the other three were plagued with power failures. MIDAS 7 operated for 47 days, and detected nine Soviet missile launches.

10th — Author Maurice Sendak, working on his first book for children, made the decision to abandon his original title, Where the Wild Horses Are, after concluding that horses were too difficult to draw, and changed the characters in the book to friendly monsters. The book, Where the Wild Things Are, would become a Caldecott Medal winning bestseller and launch Sendak's career.

12th — Scheduled to make his nationwide television debut on The Ed Sullivan Show, folk singer Bob Dylan refused to perform after censors at the CBS network wouldn't clear him to sing "Talkin' John Birch Paranoid Blues". Dylan would go on to greater fame, singing with Joan Baez in August during the "March on Washington".

14th — In Denmark, the Frederick IX Bridge was officially opened, spanning the Guldborgsund strait between the islands of Falster and Lolland.

15th — Detective James J. Hantschel of the Racine, Wisconsin Police Department was shot and killed, and another detective was shot and wounded, by a fraud suspect they were transporting to a police station.

17th — A U.S. Army OH-23 helicopter with two men on board, Captains Ben W. Stutts and Charleton W. Voltz, was shot down by North Korean ground forces after straying north of the Demilitarized Zone. The two men would be freed, after 365 days of imprisonment, on 16th May 1964, following the United Nations Command agreeing to sign a statement that Stutts and Voltz had committed espionage, but North Korea declined to return the helicopter.

20th — The World Chess Championship was won by Tigran Petrosian, who defeated world champion Mikhail Botvinnik, 12+1/2 to 9+1/2, to win the match after 22 games. The two men, both Soviet citizens, had begun play on May 23 in Moscow. Under the rules, Petrosian's five wins (worth one point each) and 15 draws (1/2 point each) brought him to 12+1/2 points first to win the series.

23rd — The first successful interception of an orbiting satellite by a ground-based missile took place as part of the American program, Project MUDFLAP. A Nike-Zeus missile, launched from Kwajalein Atoll, passed close enough to an orbiting Lockheed Agena-D satellite to have disabled it with an explosion. Seven other tests would be made, ending on 13th January 1966.

25th — At the track and field competition for six universities in what is now the Pac-12 Conference, Phil Shinnick jumped 27 feet, 4 inches in the long jump, 3/4 inch ahead of the world record set by Igor Ter-Ovanesyan, but "two officials, whose only duty was to place the wind gauge on the long jump runway and watch it to make sure the wind was blowing at less than the allowable limit, were not paying attention" so the mark was not submitted as a world record.

27th — The Freewheelin' Bob Dylan, singer-songwriter Bob Dylan's second and most influential studio album, opening with the song "Blowin' in the Wind", was released by Columbia Records.

May

28th | A cyclone killed 22,000 people in and around the city of Comilla in East Pakistan (now Bangladesh). Winds as high as 150 m.p.h. ripped the countryside, and "the many offshore islands were literally swept clean of people"; both Chittagong and Cox's Bazar lost 5,000 people each, and waves were powerful enough to send ships half a mile inland, including four ocean liners.

29th | Jim Reeves was welcomed to Ireland by show band singers Maisie McDaniel and Dermot O'Brien, at the start of his tour of Ireland, and conducted a week-long tour of U.S. military bases in England.

30th | The initial announcements were made for the first diet drink manufactured by the Coca-Cola Company, with TaB cola, with "one calorie per six-ounce serving".

31st | The ABC Theatre in Blackpool, UK, opened, beginning with the Holiday Carnival summer season stage show, starring Cliff Richard and The Shadows.

June

1st | Willie Pastrano, a 6 to 1 underdog challenger, won the world light heavyweight boxing championship, defeating titleholder Harold Johnson. Although most sportswriters thought that Johnson had won the 15-round bout in Las Vegas, Pastrano was declared the winner by the judges in a 2 to 1 decision. "I'm not saying that the underworld dictated the decision," Johnson's manager told reporters afterward, "but the betting was 5-1 and 6-1 for my boy? What do you think?"

3rd | Northwest Airlines Flight 293, a Douglas DC-7C, crashed in the Pacific Ocean west-southwest of Annette Island, Alaska, off the coast of British Columbia, Canada, killing all 101 people on board. Chartered to carry U.S. military personnel and their families from McChord Air Force Base in Washington, to Elmendorf Air Force Base in Alaska, the plane disappeared shortly after being cleared to climb to an altitude of 18,000 feet. Forty-seven years ago, the cause of the accident remained unknown and the wreckage of the airplane remained "under more than 8,000 feet of water in the Gulf of Alaska".

4th | Robert Wesley Patch, a six-year-old boy from Chevy Chase, Maryland, was awarded United States Patent No. 3,091,888 for a toy truck that could be "readily assembled and disassembled by a child".

8th | The first Titan II nuclear intercontinental ballistic missiles became operational, with the activation by the United States of a group at the Davis–Monthan Air Force Base near Tucson, Arizona.

June

10th | U.S. President Kennedy announced the suspension of nuclear testing during his commencement address at American University in Washington, D.C., along with the administration's plan to work towards a nuclear test-ban treaty with the Soviet Union and other atomic powers.

11th | The first lung transplant on a human being was performed at the University of Mississippi, by Dr. James Hardy The patient, identified twelve days later as John Richard Russell, a convicted murderer serving a life sentence for a 1957 killing, was given a full pardon Mississippi Governor Ross Barnett, in recognition of Russell's volunteering for the operation, which Barnett said would "alleviate human misery and suffering in years to come". The donor, never identified, had arrived at the hospital emergency room in the evening after having a massive heart attack, and the family permitted the donation of the left lung for transplant; Russell survived for 18 more days after the surgery.

15th | The French retailing chain Carrefour opened the first hypermarket in Europe. With 2,500 square meters of floor space for a grocery store and department store, parking space for 350 cars, and its own gasoline station, the first Carrefour hypermarket was opened at the Paris suburb of Sainte-Geneviève-des-Bois, Essonne.

17th | ASCII (United States of America Standard Code for Information Interchange) was approved by the American Standards Association, providing a seven-bit code of up to 128-character positions that could be used for communication between computer information processing systems.

19th | The Soviet Union's Mars 1 spacecraft came within 193,000 kilometres (120,000 miles) of the planet Mars, the first man-made object to reach the Red Planet, but was unable to return any data to Earth because of a malfunction in its antenna on 21st March.

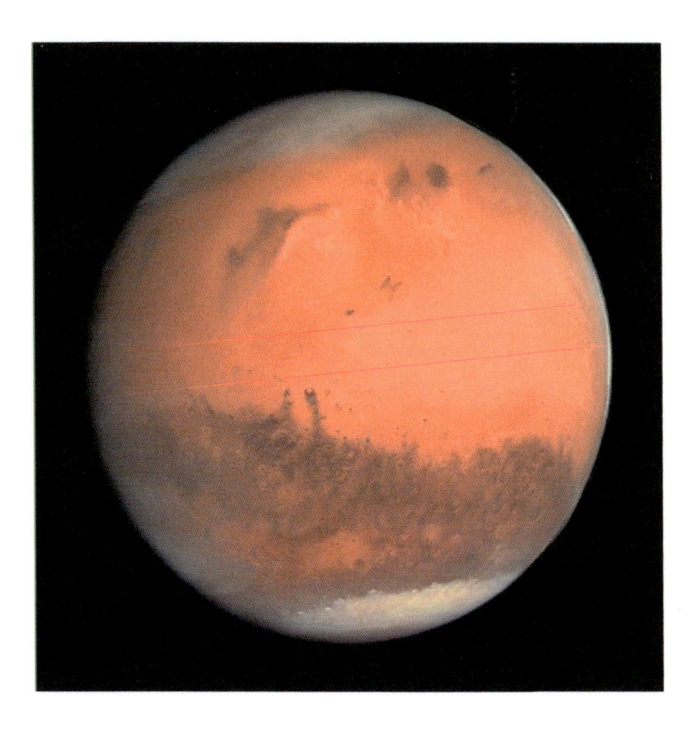

20th | The United States team won the first ever Federation Cup (tennis), defeating Australia in the finals.

21st | The 13th Berlin International Film Festival opened.

June

24th — The Telcan, the first system designed to be used at home for recording programs from a television set, was given its first demonstration. The system, shown in Nottingham, England, was seen to record programs onto a reel of videotape and then to play them back with "very fair video quality" on a 17-inch TV, could hold 30 minutes of programming, and had a suggested retail price of £60 ($175).

26th — U.S. President Kennedy delivered his famous "Ich bin ein Berliner" speech in front of the Berlin Wall in West Berlin. After climbing a specially built reviewing stand at the Brandenburg Gate so that he could look into East Berlin, Kennedy was driven to the West Berlin city hall, where he addressed a crowd of 150,000 people. Kennedy began his speech by saying that "2,000 years ago, the proudest boast was civis Romanus sum [Latin, "I am a Roman"]. Today, in the world of freedom, the proudest boast is Ich bin ein Berliner [German, "I am a Berliner"]".

27th — In a visit to Ireland, U.S. President Kennedy visited Dunganstown, which his great-grandfather Patrick Kennedy had left in 1843 to emigrate to the United States. "If he hadn't left," Kennedy joked, "I'd be working at the Albatross Company", a local fertilizer factory. Kennedy was hosted by his third cousin, widow Mary Ann Ryan.

30th — A car bomb killed five police officers and two military engineers in Italy at Ciaculli, a suburb of Palermo on the island of Sicily. A bomb that had been visible on the backseat of an Alfa Romeo car had been defused, but when a police officer opened the trunk of the automobile, a second bomb exploded. The event was the culmination of the First Mafia War, breaking the unofficial peace pact between the police and the Mafia; over the next month, 10,000 police were sent from the Italian mainland and 250 mafiosi were arrested, suspending the activities of the Cosa Nostra.

July

1st — ZIP Codes were introduced in the US, as the U.S. Department of the Post Office kicked off a massive advertising campaign that included the cartoon character "Mr. ZIP", and the mailing that day of more than 72,000,000 postcards to every mailing address in the United States, in order to inform the addressees of their new five-digit postal code. Postal zones had been used since 1943 in large cities, but the ZIP code was nationwide. Use became mandatory in 1967 for bulk mailers.

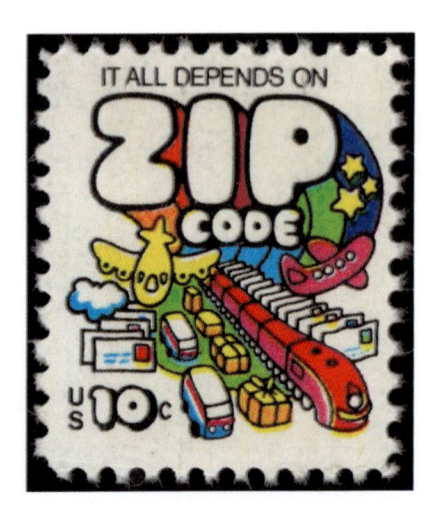

2nd — Brian Sternberg, the world record holder for the pole vault, broke his neck after falling from a trampoline, and was left a quadriplegic.

July

3rd | The 100th anniversary of the Battle of Gettysburg, turning point of the American Civil War, was celebrated with a re-enactment of Pickett's charge.

5th | The sale of liquor, by the drink, was legal in Iowa for the first time in more than 40 years, with "a restaurant in the lakes resort area in northwest Iowa" becoming the site of the first legal drink.

6th | The Vanoise National Park, located in the department of Savoie in the French Alps, was designated France's first National Park.

8th | Members of the 1963 American Everest Expedition team were awarded the Hubbard Medal by U.S. President John F. Kennedy for their achievement.

12th | The first "Gambit" military reconnaissance satellite was launched from Vandenberg Air Force Base in California at 1:44 p.m., and the film recovered proved it to be a major advancement in observation. The new system had "exceptional pointing accuracy" in aiming its cameras, and the pictures obtained had a resolution of 3.5 feet.

14th | U.S. Undersecretary of State W. Averell Harriman arrived in Moscow in order to negotiate the nuclear test ban treaty, and brought with him three tons of American telephone and telex equipment to set up the Moscow–Washington hotline agreed upon by the Americans and Soviets on 20th June.

15th | The Kingdom of Tonga issued the first-round postage stamps in history. The stamps (which were also the first to be made of gold foil rather than paper) were designed to commemorate the first gold coins in Polynesia.

17th | The final launch was made from the Cape Canaveral Air Force Station Launch Complex 21.

19th | An artificial heart pump was placed inside a human being for the first time, at the Methodist Hospital in Houston, Texas University of Houston by a team led by Dr. Michael E. DeBakey. The unidentified patient survived for four days before dying of complications from pneumonia.

July

22nd — World heavyweight boxing champion Sonny Liston retained his title in a rematch fight against former champion Floyd Patterson, whom he had defeated ten months earlier, on 20th September 1962. In the first bout, he knocked out Patterson in the first round in two minutes, six seconds. In the rematch at Las Vegas, Liston took four seconds longer.

26th — NASA launched Syncom 2, the world's first geostationary (synchronous) satellite. Synchronization would be achieved eight days later, on 3rd August with Syncom 2 reaching a point 22,500 miles above Brazil, and then moving at 6,880 miles per hour in order to keep pace with the Earth's equatorial rotational movement of 1,040 miles per hour.

29th — The Los Angeles Herald-Examiner published its copyrighted story, "Black Muslim Founder Exposed as a White", that W. D. Fard, who had started the black nationalist organization in 1930, had actually been a white man named Wallace Dodd. The Herald-Examiner story included photographs supplied by the FBI, but Fard's successors at the Nation of Islam denied the story as a hoax.

31st — Paul Foytack of the California Angels became the first Major League Baseball pitcher to surrender four consecutive home runs, during the sixth inning of a 9-5 loss to the Cleveland Indians. Only one other player accomplished the feat, when Chase Wright of the New York Yankees gave up four homers in a row in a 7-6 loss to the Boston Red Sox on 22nd April 2007.

August

2nd — The Sino-Soviet split widened as the People's Republic of China, in its strongest condemnation to that time of the Soviet Union, criticized the Soviets as being "freaks and monsters" for making "unconditional concessions and capitulation to the imperialists" after the USSR had agreed to a partial nuclear test ban treaty with the United States and the United Kingdom. The statement came in an editorial in the Chinese Communist Party newspaper, the People's Daily.

4th — The 1963 German Grand Prix was held at the Nürburgring and won by John Surtees, with Jim Clark finishing second. Clark remained well in first place in the world auto-driving championship standings, with 42 points, while Surtees was second at 22.

5th — Craig Breedlove set the record for fastest driver in the world, reaching 428.37 miles an hour "for a measured mile" in a jet-powered vehicle, Spirit of America, on the Bonneville Salt Flats in Utah. His average for two runs was 407.45 MPH.

7th — A freak escalator accident at the Garden State Park Racetrack in Cherry Hill, New Jersey, killed a man and his daughter. John Patrick Sweeney and 8-year old Peggy Sweeney, of Maple Shade, New Jersey, were touring the closed park with a friend when they stepped over a box of tools that had been blocking the moving stairway, unaware that a protective plate at the top had been removed for maintenance. The two fell into the moving machinery and were crushed to death.

10th — A new record was set for latest ending to a Major League Baseball game, when the second game of a doubleheader between the Pittsburgh Pirates, and the visiting Houston Colt .45s (now the Astros lasted until 2:30 in the morning. The first game had been delayed for an hour by rain. Only 300 of the original 9,420 fans stayed to watch Pittsburgh win 7-6 after 11 innings. The record would be broken on 13th June 1967, when a Washington Senators 6-5 win over the Chicago White Sox at 2:44 am.

August

12th — Fifteen of the 16 people on board an Air-Inter flight were killed when the Viscount airplane they were on crashed while attempting a landing in a thunderstorm at Lyon. The airplane, which was stopping at Lille on the way to Nice, struck a barn as it descended, and debris from the wreckage killed the farm owner. The sole survivor was a three-year-old girl.

16th — The NASA M2-F1, a wingless lifting body glider nicknamed the "flying bathtub", was flown for the first time, with test pilot Milt Thompson at the controls. The lifting body design, which permitted a spacecraft to descend horizontally through the atmosphere, would be put into service through the American space shuttle.

18th — The last match in the third round of the 1963 CONCACAF Champions' Cup was played at the Estadio Nacional in Costa Rica. The final, scheduled to be played the following month, would eventually be scratched, and Racing Club Haïtien would eventually be declared champion.

22nd — American test pilot Joe Walker achieved a second sub-orbital spaceflight, according to the international standard of 100 kilometres, piloting an X-15 rocket to an altitude of 354,200 feet (67.08 miles or 107.96 kilometres). The record was unofficial, because the X-15 did not take off from the ground under its own power, and sent up by an air launch. Walker's flight would remain the highest ever achieved by an airplane for more than fifty years, until broken on 4th October 2004, when Brian Binnie would pilot SpaceShipOne to an altitude of 367,500 feet (69.6 miles or 112 kilometres).

28th — At the 1963 "March on Washington" (officially, the March on Washington for Jobs and Freedom), Reverend Martin Luther King Jr. delivered his I Have A Dream speech on the steps of the Lincoln Memorial to an audience of at least 250,000 people.

30th — The audio cassette tape and the tape recorder that used it were both introduced to the public by the Philips Company, at the annual Internationale Funkausstellung Berlin, an exhibition of the latest consumer technology, in West Germany. For the next 30 years, the "cassette" would be the standard form of portable recorded music.

31st — Singapore declared its independence from the United Kingdom, with Yusof bin Ishak as the head of state (Yang di-Pertuan Negara) and Lee Kuan Yew as prime minister; sixteen days later, Singapore would join the Federation of Malaysia, but would declare independence again on 9th August 1965.

September

1st — An unidentified visitor to Lenin's Mausoleum, in Moscow, entered the shrine with a bomb concealed under his coat, and then detonated the explosive, killing himself and causing an unspecified amount of damage and injuries. The event was not reported in the Soviet press and would not be revealed until after the breakup of the Soviet Union.

6th — The 100,000th American major league baseball game was played, the milestone having been calculated by baseball historians from the first official game, played on 4th May 1871 by the National Association of Professional Base Ball Players. In game number 100,000 the Washington Senators defeated the visiting Cleveland Indians, 7 to 2 In the 1871 season opener, the Fort Wayne Kekiongas had defeated the visiting Cleveland Forest City team, 2 to 0.

10th — Italian Mafia boss Bernardo Provenzano was indicted for murder. Eight days later, he would become a fugitive and would not be captured until 43 years later, on 11th April 2006.

11th — A chartered Vickers 610 Viking airplane, flying from London to Perpignan, France, crashed into the side of the Roc de la Roquette, a mountain in the Pyrenees Range, killing all 40 people on board. All 36 passengers were British tourists. Earlier in the day, another Vickers airplane, and Indian Airlines Viscount turboprop, crashed while en route from Nagpur to New Delhi, killing all 18 people on board.

13th — Mary Kay Cosmetics was incorporated by a Texas widow, Mary Kay Ash, who invested her life savings of $5,000. By the time of her death in 2001, the company had sales of $1.4 billion.

16th — The science fiction anthology television show, The Outer Limits, premiered on the ABC television network at 7:30 pm in the United States, beginning with the episode "The Galaxy Being".

18th — The last sports event took place at the Polo Grounds in New York City, with baseball's New York Mets losing to the Philadelphia Phillies, 5-1 before a crowd of only 1,752 people. When the game ended, the fans ran onto the field, vandalizing the scoreboard and the sod on the field, as well as some of the seats in the stadium, which was scheduled to be torn down in 1964.

20th — The first successful prenatal blood transfusion in history was performed in New Zealand at the National Women's Hospital at Auckland. Dr. William Liley carried out the transfusion on the unborn son of a woman identified only as "Mrs. E. McLeod" in order to treat the fetus for hemolytic disease. The baby was born later in the day.

22nd — South Korea began its commitment to the Vietnam War, sending the first of 312,853 soldiers who would fight against the North Vietnamese.

24th — Eighteen people were killed and twelve seriously injured in the explosion of a fireworks factory at the Italian city of Caserta. The factory owner, who was killed in the blast, had reportedly been asking the employees to rush to produce additional fireworks for the festival of Saint Michael the Archangel.

27th — According to the Warren Commission, Lee Harvey Oswald arrived in Mexico City on this date and went to the consulate of Cuba, where he applied for a transit visa to travel to Cuba and then back to the Soviet Union, where he had lived from 1959 to 1962. After being refused visas by the Cuban consulate and the Soviet embassy, the Commission concluded, Oswald returned to his home near Dallas, Texas after a few days.

October

1st	The Sand War began when troops from Morocco invaded Algeria and seized control of two oases that had served as border stations on the road to Tindouf. Algeria retook the oases a week later, but Morocco took them back the week after that, and then expand its control of territory in western Algeria until a peace treaty could be brokered.
3rd	Hurricane Flora reached its highest wind speed, with winds of 200 miles per hour, and made landfall at Haiti, where it took its highest toll. Over the next three days, 75 inches of rain fell, 5,000 Haitians were killed and 100,000 people were left homeless. Although the storm had been spotted seven days earlier, Haitian Red Cross Director Jacques Fourcand and President Francois Duvalier had prohibited the radio broadcast of any warnings, as a measure to "reduce panic". The hurricane "spend five days crossing and re-crossing Cuba" and killed 1,000 people there.
4th	U.S. First Lady Jacqueline Kennedy arrived for a visit in Greece as the guest of shipping magnate Aristotle Onassis. Following the assassination of President Kennedy, the former First Lady married Onassis as her second husband.
6th	Surf music, performed primarily in Southern California, received its first nationwide American television exposure, when Dick Dale and the Del-Tones appeared on The Ed Sullivan Show.
8th	Black artist Sam Cooke, his wife, and two members of his band were arrested after trying to register at a "whites only" motel in Shreveport, Louisiana. The charge of disturbing the peace came after the clerk told police that Cooke had continuously blown his car horn after being told that the motel was closed. That incident, and the tragic drowning of his 18-month old son earlier in the year, led Cooke to record the classic on 17th June song "A Change Is Gonna Come". Cooke was shot and killed at another motel in Los Angeles on 11th December 1964.
10th	After conferring with FBI Director J. Edgar Hoover, U.S. Attorney General Robert F. Kennedy approved wiretapping and other surveillance of the home of Dr. Martin Luther King Jr. and the New York City office of the Southern Christian Leadership Conference. Listening devices were installed in the New York office on 24th October and in Dr. King's home on 8th November.
16th	The first pair of "Vela" satellites, designed to detect nuclear bomb detonations on Earth, were launched from Cape Canaveral, Florida at 9:33 pm. The satellites were placed in an orbit 60,000 miles above the Earth's surface, in order to verify compliance with the Nuclear Test Ban Treaty that had recently gone into effect. The Vela program continued until 8th April 1970, when the last of the 12 detection satellites were put into space.
18th	Meeting at Baden-Baden in West Germany, the International Olympic Committee awarded the 1968 Olympic Games to Mexico City. The other three candidates that had submitted bids had been Detroit, Lyons and Buenos Aires.
21st	Cuba began a large-scale military presence in Africa, with the arrival of the first of 2,200 soldiers and 1,000 advisers at Algeria. Commanded by General Efigenio Ameijeiras, the group (along with fifty T-55 tanks and several MiG-17 fighters) was brought on three merchant ships to the port of Oran in order to assist in the war against Morocco.
23rd	The Spanish ship SS Juan Ferrer capsized and sank near Boscawen Point, United Kingdom with the loss of 11 of the 15 crew.

October

26th | Soviet Prime Minister Nikita Khrushchev announced, through the publication of an interview in the government newspaper Izvestia, that the Soviets were not going to compete with the United States in the race to put the first man on the Moon. "At the present time, we do not plan flights of cosmonauts to the Moon," he said. "I have read a report that the Americans wish to land a man on the Moon by 1970. Well, let's wish them success."

27th | Jimmy Tarbuck made his first appearance at the London Palladium.

29th | Hurricane Ginny reached peak winds of 110 mph (175 km/h), subsequently becoming extratropical before making landfall on southwestern Nova Scotia, Canada.

November

1st | At 1:15 pm in Saigon, three marine battalions of the South Vietnam began their seizure of communications throughout the capital city, taking control of the city's radio stations, national and municipal police stations, and the public and Defence Ministry telecommunications centres. The acts were the first in a coup d'état against President Ngo Dinh Diem and his brother Ngo Dinh Nhu. The planners had set a deadline of 1:15 to either begin the coup or to call it off, and were waiting until visiting U.S. Admiral Harry Felt had departed. Admiral Felt's airplane took off at 1:00 pm. Diem and Nhu quietly escaped Gia Long Palace by 8:00 p.m. and fled to refuge at the Roman Catholic church in the nearby Cholon section of the city.

6th | In Midland, Texas, 17-year old Laura Welch, who would later marry George W. Bush and become the First Lady upon his inauguration as President of the United States, ran a stop sign at the intersection of Farm Road 868 and Big Spring Street, and crashed into the side of a car driven by one of her classmates at Robert E. Lee High School, 17-year old Michael Dutton Douglas. Laura Bush would finally write about the accident after her husband left office, in her 2010 memoir, spoken from the Heart, recounting that she and her friend were hurrying to a drive-in movie. Douglas, whose neck was broken, died at the local hospital.

11th | The first interplanetary probe in the Soviet Union's Zond program, designated Kosmos 21, failed to escape Earth orbit after a misfiring of a rocket and a failure of proper attitude control.

November

13th — Two hours after Radio Baghdad announced that Syria's Ba'athist Party was now led by Prime Minister Ahmed Hassan al-Bakr, the station was taken off of the air by supporters of recently deposed leader Ali Salih al-Sadi, Iraqi fighter jets strafed the Presidential Palace, and thousands of demonstrators protested the shakeup. Premier al-Bakr and eight of the new 15-member Ba'athist council were overthrown and sent into exile in Beirut, Lebanon, the next day.

15th — The new island of Surtsey was created off of the coast of Iceland by the eruption of an undersea volcano, and was first spotted by the crew of the Isleifur II, a fishing boat from Iceland. By 5th June 1967, upon the halt of the eruption, the island would have an area of 2.8 square kilometres (1.08 square miles).

18th — The first touch-tone phone was released to the public. This signalled the end of the rotary phone, since it was easier to dial.

21st — India began its space program with the launching of a sounding rocket from the Thumba Equatorial Rocket Launching Station (TERLS), located at the far south end of the Indian subcontinent, near Thiruvananthapuram in the Kerala State. The rocket test took place 25 minutes after sunset, and reached an altitude of 200 kilometres (124 miles) where it released a sodium vapor cloud in the thermosphere.

22nd — U.S. President John F. Kennedy was assassinated in Dallas, Texas, while he was riding as a passenger in a Lincoln Continental convertible automobile. He was accompanied by his wife, Jacqueline Kennedy, Texas Governor John Connally and the Governor's wife Nellie Connally, Secret Service Agent Roy Kellerman, and the driver, agent William Greer. The group was part of several cars in a motorcade of vehicles on the way from the Dallas airport, Love Field, to the Dallas Trade Mart, where the President was scheduled to deliver a speech at a luncheon for 2,600 guests. At 12:30 p.m., as their car was passing in front of the Texas School Book Depository at 411 Elm Street, President Kennedy and Governor Connally were struck by bullets fired at long range. The President arrived at the Parkland Memorial Hospital at 12:38 p.m. and was taken into surgery, and pronounced dead at 1:00 p.m.

25th — The state funeral of John F. Kennedy took place in Washington, D.C., as the late President's casket was transported in the funeral procession to the Arlington National Cemetery.

December

1st — Malcolm X described the Kennedy assassination as a case of America's "chickens coming home to roost", resulting in his suspension on 4th December and eventual excommunication from the Nation of Islam.

2nd — What has been called "the first mixed martial arts match of the modern age" took place in Salt Lake City, Utah, when judo champion and professional wrestler Gene LeBell accepted a challenge to fight light heavyweight boxer Milo Savage, who was ranked fifth in the world at the time. LeBell, responding to a $1,000 challenge that no judo practitioner could defeat a boxer in a fight, defeated Savage in the fourth round by choking him and rendering him unconscious. The match itself, staged before 1,500 people was billed as a "boxer vs. judo man" program.

6th — Two weeks after the assassination of President Kennedy, former First Lady Jacqueline Kennedy, her daughter Caroline and her son John, Jr., moved out of the White House shortly after noon. President Johnson and his wife, Lady Bird Johnson, had agreed that the Kennedy family could have as much time as they needed to pack up their belongings and move to a different home. Mrs. Kennedy and her children then moved into a townhouse in nearby Georgetown, loaned to them by Undersecretary of State W. Averell Harriman. On their last full day in the White House, John Jr.'s birthday party, postponed because 25th November had been the day of his father's funeral, was celebrated. Caroline continued to attend her first-grade class with friends at the White House until the end of the year, after which the school was disbanded.

7th — Americans got their first glimpse of the new British music group, The Beatles, when a clip of one of their performances (and the enthusiastic support from the British fans) was shown on the CBS Evening News. Radio stations in the U.S. began receiving requests to play Beatles songs, and several began to import copies from the U.K.

8th — Frank Sinatra Jr., the 19-year-old son of the famous singer, was kidnapped from his Room 417 at Harrah's Lake Tahoe in Stateline, Nevada. Three men, Barry Keenan, John Irwin and Joe Amsler, entered the room at 9:30 p.m., half an hour before the younger Sinatra was to open a show with the Tommy Dorsey band, forced him into their car, and then drugged him and drove him to Canoga Park, California. From there, they called the elder Sinatra and demanded $240,000 ransom. The amount of $239,985 was dropped off in a small suitcase, and the kidnap victim was released, unharmed, on the San Diego Freeway, in the early morning hours of 11th December. The three kidnappers would all be released by 1968.

10th — Future pop singer and teen idol Donny Osmond made his national television debut at the age of six, joining his older brothers as guests on The Andy Williams Show.

14th — At 3:38 in the afternoon, an earthen dam gave way, sending one million cubic meters (300 million gallons) of water from a city reservoir down into the Los Angeles suburb of Baldwin Hills, California. More than four hours earlier, the dam' caretaker reported an unusual amount of water flowing over the spillway and notified Los Angeles Department of Water Resources engineers and safety officials. Evacuation of the suburb of 16,500 residents began while an attempt was made to slow the leakage with sandbags, but by 1:30, a one-fifth inch wide crack in the wall began to widen. By 1:45, the gap had increased to three inches, and the downstream side of the dam began to leak by 2:00. By 3:15 the break had widened to nearly 10 feet and the dam burst 23 minutes later. More than 200 homes were destroyed but, because of the evacuation, only five people were killed in the disaster.

December

17th	The Clean Air Act of 1963 was signed into law by President Johnson.
20th	The manufacture of Studebaker automobiles in the United States came to a halt as the company's factory in South Bend, Indiana, closed permanently and its last product— a red Studebaker Daytona hardtop— was completed on the assembly line, and the plant's 6,000 workers were laid off. Canadian production of Studebakers would continue in Hamilton, Ontario for a little more than two years afterward, until 16th March 1966.
21st	TIROS-8 was launched into orbit, and became the first weather satellite to relay digital images back to Earth at the same time that they were being recorded, using the new technology of automatic picture transmission. The first photos were sent to Earth at 11:30 a.m. Eastern time as it passed over the east coast of the United States on its fourth orbit, and showed the cloud cover along the Atlantic seaboard.
22nd	Paul Robeson returned to the United States after a self-imposed exile of five years, most of it in the Soviet Union. The African-American singer, former football star and Communist activist, had departed the U.S. in 1958 after a nine-year fight for an American passport.
23rd	Top FBI officials, led by Assistant Director William C. Sullivan, met at the Washington headquarters to discuss plans for "neutralizing Martin Luther King Jr. as an effective Negro leader", primarily by using wiretapping of hotel rooms to gather evidence of his extramarital affairs, and then to leak the tapes to the press.
25th	Walt Disney released his 18th feature-length animated motion picture, The Sword in the Stone, about the boyhood of King Arthur. It would be the penultimate animated film personally supervised by Disney.
26th	Israel entered a new phase in its atomic weapons research program when it activated its first nuclear reactor at its Negev Nuclear Research Centre at Dimona. An American inspection team would learn of the development about three weeks later, on January 18, but would find no evidence of plutonium or irradiated uranium at that time and conclude that Israel had "no weapons making capability".
28th	TV Malaysia began broadcasting from Kuala Lumpur as "The First Channel" and the first such station in that city, televising programs in black and white. At the time, Singapore, with two television stations, was still part of Malaysia, until its separation in 1964, "The First Channel" would become the only Malaysian station.
29th	Twenty-one people were killed when the 13-story Roosevelt Hotel caught fire in Jacksonville, Florida. Because the fire had started in the hotel ballroom, escape to the ground floor quickly became impossible, but another 14 guests made their way to the hotel roof and were rescued by U.S. Navy helicopters from the Naval Air Stations at Cecil Field and the Jacksonville NAS.
30th	U.S. President Johnson signed a bill authorizing the minting of a new version of the Kennedy half dollar, with the profile of John F. Kennedy on the obverse and the U.S. presidential seal on the other side. The new fifty cent piece replaced the coin with the images of Benjamin Franklin and the Liberty Bell, with the first coins being minted simultaneously on 11th February 1964, at the mints in Philadelphia and Denver.

PEOPLE IN POWER

Robert Menzies
1949-1966
Australia
Prime Minister

Charles de Gaulle
1959-1969
France
Président

João Goulart
1961-1964
Brazil
President

John Diefenbaker
1957-1963
Canada
Prime Minister

Mao Zedong
1943-1976
China
Government of China

Heinrich Lübke
1959-1969
Germany
President of Germany

Sarvepalli Radhakrishnan
1962-1967
India
1st President of India

Antonio Segni
1962-1964
Italy
President

Hiroito
1926-1989
Japan
Emperor

Adolfo López Mateos
1958-1964
Mexico
President of Mexico

Nikita Khrushchev
1958-1964
Russia
Premier

Hendrik Verwoerd
1958-1966
South Africa
Prime Minister

John F. Kennedy
1961-1963
United States
President

Théo Lefèvre
1961-1965
Belgium
Prime Minister

Keith Holyoake
1960-1972
New Zealand
Prime Minister

Harold Macmillan
1957-1963
United Kingdom
Prime Minister

Tage Erlander
1946-1969
Sweden
Prime Minister

Jens Otto Krag
1962-1968
Denmark
Prime Minister

Francisco Franco
1936-1975
Spain
President

János Kádár
1961-1965
Hungary
Hungarian Working
People's Party

The Year You Were Born 1963
Book by Sapphire Publishing
All rights reserved

Printed in Great Britain
by Amazon